Nuclear Weapons

by William Lambers

Cover photograph: ROMEO, an 11 megaton shot, part of Operation Castle on March 26, 1954. (courtesy U.S. Department of Energy)

Nuclear Weapons
Third Edition, ISBN: 0965652076
Copyright © 2002, 2001 by William Lambers

Printed in the United States of America

www.lamberspublications.com

TABLE OF CONTENTS

Chapter One
The Atomic Bomb

Imagine yourself an American soldier stationed in the Pacific during World War II. You are a part of an allied force preparing to invade Japan. No doubt it will be the final battle of the war, a war that began over three years earlier with the surprise Japanese attack on Pearl Harbor, which killed or wounded thousands of Americans. The fighting on the islands surrounding Japan has been ferocious and you know it will be more so on the Japanese mainland. You wait anxiously for the final orders to disembark on the invasion.

Picture yourself a Japanese civilian or soldier on the mainland at that same time. Despite massive allied bombing, your country will not surrender to the enemy. An American and allied ground invasion seems inevitable. Little do you know that a secret weapon is being prepared, more powerful than anything used during the war, that will decimate your country. It will fall from out of the sky and its fiery, explosive blast will kill thousands of people instantly and leave a path of destruction for miles around. Not only will this weapon cause death and destruction on its initial blast, its effects will cause sickness and death for many years to come. It will be a weapon that will strike fear into the hearts of people for generations. The weapon is the atomic bomb.

It should come as little surprise that the event that brought forward this weapon of mass destruction was the Second World War. Sole possession of the atomic bomb would be a decisive advantage for any of the warring nations. It was a matter of survival to develop the most destructive weapon conceivable. World War II had been the horrifying showcase of the most advanced, powerful and deadly weapons ever unleashed. The atomic bomb was the culmination of the most brutal conflict in the history of the world.

The early years of World War II saw Nazi Germany capture much of Europe and successfully drive deep into Russia. Japan's conquests in the Pacific added vast territory to their empire. These

German troops invading Czechoslovakia in 1938 (Getty Pictures)

Headlines tell of the German invasion of Poland in 1939. (Getty Pictures)

The USS Arizona in flames following the Japanese attack on Pearl Harbor on December 7, 1941. Following the attack, the United States declared war on Japan and also entered the war in Europe against Germany. (National Archives)

formidable foes, were they to acquire nuclear weapons, would put the U.S. and its allies in an even more precarious position.

The fear was that Germany, in particular, could develop an atomic weapon. They had rolled over nation after nation in the early years of the war before being stopped in the Battle of Britain. With their newly acquired territory came access to natural resources necessary for the creation of the bomb. In German-occupied Czechoslovakia lay uranium. German scientists had conducted research into using atomic energy to create a weapon of mass destruction. It would take time to develop such a weapon, but how much time?

United States military intelligence was keeping a close eye on the Germans.

> "...staff officers from Washington arrived at my headquarters to give me the latest calculations concerning German progress in the development of new weapons, including as possibilities bacteriological and atomic weapons.........We sent intermittent raids against every spot in Europe where the scientists believed that the Germans were attempting either to manufacture new types of weapons or where they were building launching facilities along the coast."[1]

> Dwight D. Eisenhower
> Supreme Allied Commander In Europe

Great Britain and the United States were also engaged in research and development. The United States stepped up its efforts to develop the atomic bomb with the Manhattan Project in 1942. Scientists and army personnel would soon conduct top-secret research at the Los Alamos Laboratory in New Mexico. Major General Leslie R. Groves was in charge of the Manhattan Project, which included a team of notable scientists led by Robert Oppenheimer. While the war raged on in Europe and in the Pacific,

---

[1] Eisenhower, Dwight D., "Crusade in Europe," Johns Hopkins University Press. 1997 p. 229-230

October 11, 1941.

My dear Mr. Churchill:-

It appears desirable that we should soon correspond or converse concerning the subject which is under study by your MAUD committee, and by Dr. Bush's organization in this country, in order that any extended efforts may be coordinated or even jointly conducted. I suggest, for identification, that we refer to this subject as MAUDSON.

I send this message by Mr. Hovde, head of the London office of our scientific organization, as he can, if necessary, identify the subject more explicitly, or answer your questions concerning the form of organization by which it is now being handled in this country.

With every good wish,

Always sincerely,

The Honorable
    Winston Churchill,
        Prime Minister of Great Britain,
            10 Downing Street,
                London,
                    England.

This is a letter written in October of 1941 from U.S. President Franklin Roosevelt to British Prime Minister Winston Churchill. It refers to the research being conducted by both Britain and the U.S. that would ultimately lead to the development of the atomic bomb. At the time this letter was written, Germany had driven deep into Russia and the war in the Pacific against Japan had yet to begin. (Franklin D. Roosevelt Library)

work proceeded to develop a weapon that would guarantee a United States victory.

However, the atomic bomb would not be a factor in the war in Europe. By 1945 Germany was all but defeated by the United States and its allies. In May of that year the Nazis officially surrendered. Germany had failed to develop an atomic bomb.

The war continued in the Pacific theater with Japan refusing to surrender, despite defeat after defeat, to the U.S. and its allies. Most of the territory Japan had gained early in the war was taken back by the allies. Without a Japanese surrender, it appeared inevitable that American and allied troops would have to invade the Japanese mainland. It would likely be the most horrific battle of the war, with the casualties expected to be staggering for both sides, soldiers and civilians alike. But what was to take place on July 16th, 1945 would change everything, not only for World War II but for the rest of the century and beyond.

The first atomic bomb was detonated in New Mexico. The United States had successfully developed the ultimate weapon.

The first atomic bomb test, "Trinity," on July 16, 1945 near Alamogordo, New Mexico. (National Archives)

Now that weapon could be used to end the war, thus making an invasion of Japan unnecessary. It was estimated that an invasion would cause more casualties on both sides than the dropping of the atomic bombs. On July 26[th,] the Potsdam Declaration issued by the allies demanded the unconditional surrender of Japan. However, refusing to surrender, the Japanese continued to fight on, despite heavy conventional bombing from the allies. The President of the United States, Harry S. Truman, made the decision to use the atomic bomb. But by no means did top-ranking officials unanimously agree with unleashing this weapon of mass destruction. Dwight D. Eisenhower was among the dissenters. He wrote in his memoirs of a 1945 meeting with Secretary of War Henry L. Stimson. In this meeting Stimson informed Eisenhower of preparations to use an atomic bomb against Japan.

> "………so I voiced to him my grave misgivings, first on the basis of my belief that Japan was already defeated and that dropping the bomb was completely unnecessary, and secondly because I thought that our country should avoid shocking world opinion by the use of a weapon whose employment was, I thought, no longer mandatory as a measure to save American lives."[2]

> Dwight D. Eisenhower

On August 6th, the United States dropped the atomic bomb on the Japanese city of Hiroshima.[3] Three days later, the Japanese still had not surrendered and a second atomic bomb was dropped on the city of Nagasaki. The war came to an end. It would now become another brutal chapter in the history of mankind. A new chapter would begin with the dawning of the atomic age and with it would come the terror of nuclear weapons.

---

[2] Eisenhower, Dwight D., "Mandate for Change," Doubleday Publishing, 1963, pages 312-313.

[3] For a detailed report of the atomic bombings of Hiroshima and Nagasaki see p.75.

Smoke from the blast over Hiroshima on August 6, 1945 (National Archives)

Survivors after the atomic bombing of Nagasaki, Japan (National Archives)

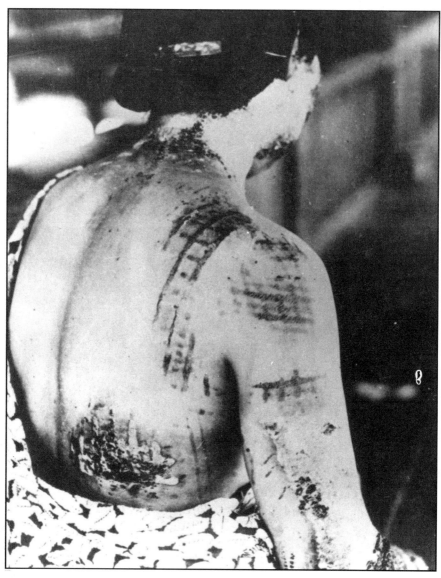

An atomic bomb survivor in Japan. "The patient's skin is burned in a pattern corresponding to the dark portions of a kimono worn at the time of the explosion." (National Archives)

Battered religious figures stand watch on a hill above a shattered valley in Nagasaki, Japan (National Archives)

HARRY S. TRUMAN

INDEPENDENCE, MISSOURI

August 5, 1963

Dear Kup:

I appreciated most highly your column of July 30th, a copy of which you sent me.

I have been rather careful not to comment on the articles that have been written on the dropping of the bomb for the simple reason that the dropping of the bomb was completely and thoroughly explained in my Memoirs, and it was done to save 125,000 youngsters on the American side and 125,000 on the Japanese side from getting killed and that is what it did. It probably also saved a half million youngsters on both sides from being maimed for life.

You must always remember that people forget, as you said in your column, that the bombing of Pearl Harbor was done while we were at peace with Japan and trying our best to negotiate a treaty with them.

All you have to do is to go out and stand on the keel of the Battleship in Pearl Harbor with the 3,000 youngsters underneath it who had no chance whatever of saving their lives. That is true of two or three other battleships that were sunk in Pearl Harbor. Altogether, there were between 3,000 and 6,000 youngsters killed at that time without any declaration of war. It was plain murder.

I knew what I was doing when I stopped the war that would have killed a half million youngsters on both sides if those bombs had not been dropped. I have no regrets and, under the same circumstances, I would do it again - and this letter is not confidential.

Sincerely yours,

Harry Truman

President Harry S. Truman defends his decision on dropping the atomic bomb in an unsent letter to Chicago newspaper columnist Irv Kupcinet (Harry S. Truman Library)

Chapter Two
Nuclear Weapons and the Cold War

While the tragedy of World War II finally did come to a conclusion with the dropping of the atomic bomb, a new struggle was beginning. The Soviet Union and the United States, who were allies in the fight against Germany and Japan, now became bitter rivals. The "Cold War" would begin. While not a direct military confrontation, it was a struggle between the two superpowers that played itself out in nearly every corner of the globe. The U.S. and the Soviet Union each had their own vision of the post-war world, particularly in nations such as Poland and Germany. In an address to the joint session of the U.S. Congress in March of 1945, President Franklin Roosevelt discussed the issue of Poland.

> *"Throughout history, Poland has been the corridor through which attacks on Russia have been made. Twice in this generation (World War I and World War II), Germany has struck at Russia through this corridor. To insure European security and world peace, a strong and independent Poland is necessary to prevent that from happening again."*

Where the Soviet Union disagreed with the United States on this issue was in the area of a strong and independent Poland. The Soviets believed control over Poland was a better way of insuring their security and world peace. Therefore, they were opposed to democracy in Poland. The Soviet Union sought control of Eastern Europe as a whole and resisted American ideas of freedom for those nations.

Still reeling from the devastation of World War II, the Soviet Union did not want to see Germany regain its strength in the post-war years.

"We understand the Russian need to be secure on her western frontiers by the removal of all possibility of German aggression."[4]

Winston Churchill

While the Russian needs for security were understood, it did not prevent a conflict over what to do with post-war Germany. Germany would end up being divided into two republics. The Soviet Union would control East Germany, while West Germany would be aligned with the United States and its allies. A wall was built, literally and figuratively, between East and West Germany and this symbolized the Cold War.

The United States sought to halt the spread of Communism, the ideology of the Soviet Union that featured strict government control on almost every aspect of life. With Eastern Europe largely under Soviet Communist influence after World War II, the United States sought to prevent its further expansion.

"I do not believe that Soviet Russia desires war. What they desire is the fruits of war and the indefinite expansion of their power and doctrines."[5]

Winston Churchill

In 1949 the North Atlantic Treaty Organization (NATO) was founded to serve as a shield against Soviet expansion. The NATO alliance consisted of the United States, Canada and many Western European nations.

And then the plot would thicken. In September of 1949 evidence of an unidentified atomic explosion was uncovered. A U.S. Air Force memo stated the source of the blast as "over the Asiatic Land Mass" occurring between August 26th and the 29th.[6]

---

[4] The quote is from Winston Churchill's speech "The Sinews of Peace," March 5, 1946.

[5] Ibid

[6] Memorandum by the Chief of Staff, U.S. Air Force to the Secretary of Defense on Long Range Detection of Atomic Explosions (see Appendix page 125)

14

Scientists from the U.S. and Britain confirmed their glum findings. The Soviet Union had tested its first atomic bomb. The inevitable had become a reality, although sooner than many had expected. Soviet Premier Josef Stalin had made it a priority that his nation would have the same destructive firepower as the United States.

Nuclear weapons, weapons of mass destruction, would become a centerpiece of the "Cold War." By outdoing the other in nuclear superiority, a decided advantage could be gained in the Cold War. The Soviet Union and the United States were the most powerful nations militarily in the world. During the next several decades, each would develop thousands upon thousands of nuclear weapons, enough weapons to destroy the world many times over.

The nuclear weapons race would take off in the 1950's with the development of nuclear weapons much more powerful than those unleashed on Japan in WWII. The more powerful hydrogen bomb was first tested by the United States in 1952 and the Soviets were not far behind in testing their own the following year.

One could, perhaps naively, think that the death and destruction of World War II would have been the war to end all wars. What greater tragedy to befall civilization than the Second World War? But instead of world peace, there was division and conflict. There were small regional conflicts erupting throughout the world, and in June of 1950 Communist North Korea attacked South Korea, and the fighting would last for three years.

In 1952 the United States elected Dwight D. Eisenhower as their president. He was a leader who knew full well about military strength, having been the Supreme Allied Commander in Europe during the Second World War. He would preside over a massive nuclear arms buildup during the two terms of his presidency, while the Soviets engaged in their own efforts. He would also be a leader in the call for world peace and the use of atomic energy for peaceful, rather than destructive, purposes. In April of 1953 President Eisenhower gave the speech, "The Chance for Peace." It was only eight years earlier that the United States and the Soviet Union were allies in the war against Nazi Germany. Now they were at odds. An excerpt from President Eisenhower's speech, "The Chance for Peace".....

"In that spring of victory the soldiers of the Western Allies met the soldiers of Russia in the center of Europe. They were triumphant comrades in arms. Their peoples shared the joyous prospect of building, in honor of their dead, the only fitting monument--an age of just peace. All of these war-weary peoples shared too this concrete, decent purpose: to guard vigilantly against the domination ever again of any part of the world by a single, unbridled aggressive power. This common purpose lasted an instant and perished."

Picture of the historic meeting of Russian and American armies near Torgau, Germany in 1945 prior to the end of the war in Europe. Soon afterward the Cold War and a massive nuclear arms race between the two nations would begin. (National Archives)

President Eisenhower also commented on the futility of a nuclear arms race.

> "A nation's hope of lasting peace cannot be firmly based upon any race in armaments but rather upon just relations and honest understanding with all other nations."

> "Every gun that is made, every warship launched, every rocket fired signifies, in the final sense, a theft from those who hunger and are not fed, those who are cold and are not clothed."

A 1953 report from the U.S. National Security Council estimated the number of casualties from an all-out Soviet nuclear attack at 31,000,000 (see pages 18-20). A horrific scenario, to say the least, but it gets worse. The weapons stockpiles of each nation would continue to grow larger in the years following that assessment. In addition, the means of delivering nuclear weapons would become more abundant and proficient. Soon the Soviet Union and the United States would have the capability of launching nuclear missiles that could strike virtually any target in the world.

Air Force Consolidated SM-65 "Atlas" Intercontinental Ballistic Missile after launch from Cape Canaveral in Florida (National Archives)

THE FOLLOWING PAGES CONTAIN EXCERPTS FROM A REPORT BY A
SUBCOMMITTEE OF THE U.S. NATIONAL SECURITY COUNCIL. THE REPORT
EVALUATES THE CAPABILITY OF THE SOVIET UNION TO INFLICT DAMAGE ON THE
UNITED STATES UP TO JULY 1, 1955. NOTE THE SIZE OF THE SOVIET
UNION'S ARSENAL OF ATOMIC WEAPONS UNDER THE "SOVIET CAPABILITIES"
SECTION. PARAGRAPH 46 ESTIMATES THE CASUALTIES FROM AN ATOMIC BOMB
ATTACK. (NSC 140/1 COURTESY OF THE EISENHOWER LIBRARY)

NSC 140/1

~~TOP SECRET~~
SECURITY INFORMATION
SPECIAL SECURITY HANDLING

COPY NO. 1

A REPORT

TO THE

NATIONAL SECURITY COUNCIL

by

THE SPECIAL EVALUATION SUBCOMMITTEE OF THE NSC

on

SUMMARY EVALUATION OF THE NET CAPABILITY OF THE USSR TO INFLICT
DIRECT INJURY ON THE UNITED STATES UP TO JULY 1, 1955

May 18, 1953

WASHINGTON

~~TOP SECRET~~

DISCUSSION

I.   SOVIET CAPABILITIES

1.   On the basis of the latest agreed intelligence estimates, we have made the following evaluations of Soviet capabilities:

A.   Mass Destruction Weapons

2.   Atomic Weapons: The USSR's stockpile of atomic weapons is estimated to consist of approximately the following numbers of weapons of about 80 KT power:

> Mid-1953   120
> Mid-1955   300

The USSR probably can make weapons of smaller or larger yield than those indicated above and in so doing would increase or reduce the number of weapons in stockpile. We believe that the USSR will not have a deliverable thermonuclear weapon or significant quantities of radiological warfare agents during the period under review.

3.   Biological Weapons: The USSR will probably possess a capability to produce and disseminate virulent biological agents on a limited scale.

4.   Chemical Weapons: The USSR will probably possess the capability to engage in large-scale chemical warfare using World War II-type standard chemical agents. By mid-1955, the USSR will probably possess limited stocks of nerve gas.

B.   Capability to Deliver By Aircraft

5.   Strength of Long-Range Aviation: In mid-1953, the USSR will probably possess about 1000 medium bombers of the TU-4 type (comparable to the US B-29). By mid-1955, this number may be increased to about 1100. Also, by mid-1955, the USSR may have as many as 180 heavy bombers with a range about twice that of the TU-4. While the TU-4 might be considered an obsolescent aircraft as compared with modern bomber aircraft now operational in the U.S. Air Force, it does have comparative range, load-carrying capacity, and reliability. It also has considerable capability for operations during darkness and under conditions of poor visibility.

160

19

D. Vulnerability of General Economic Strengths, Population, and Governmental Control Complexes

45. There are 169 urban areas in the United States with a population of 50,000 or more. Of these urban areas, 54 are major metropolitan industrial areas or government control centers with a population of about 200,000 or more. These 54 complexes contain 71 percent of the country's war industry and 35 percent of the country's population. They also contain the nerve centers of economic and governmental control.

46. In mid-1953, if the USSR launched virtually its entire atomic weapons stockpile against those urban areas in the United States with the greatest population densities, and if it succeeded in attacking without warning and in achieving optimum placement, it has been estimated that casualties as high as 24,000,000 might be inflicted. In mid-1955, the same kind of attack under the same conditions with the larger stockpile might produce personnel casualties as high as 31,000,000. It is estimated that casualties would be reduced by approximately one-half with one hour warning. About one-half of the casualties would result in deaths. In such attacks, designed primarily to produce casualties, there would also be serious industrial damage, widespread dislocation of our highly integrated economic and social systems, loss of morale, panic, defeatism, etc., in amounts and to degrees which it is impossible to measure on the basis of any presently available valid data.

47. These population, industrial, and control centers are largely in the northeastern part of the United States, in the northern Middle West, and in the coastal areas. They are, therefore, on the periphery of the defended area and are of such size in themselves as to offer targets which could most easily and successfully, of all areas in the United States, be brought under attack by the inexperienced Soviet long-range bomber force.

48. While the net effect of a successful attack cannot be estimated with acceptable accuracy, at a minimum, it would disrupt the governmental control system, it would strain the civil defense system far beyond its present capabilities, and it would necessitate a prolonged rehabilitation effort. The U.S. retaliatory force itself, however, would be relatively intact and would be able to carry out its prescribed mission. There would be no physical reason why it could not deliver heavy and devastating retaliatory blows against the USSR.

20

Chapter Three
Atoms for Peace

Later that same year, President Eisenhower would make his "Atoms for Peace" speech which would pave the way for the creation of the International Atomic Energy Agency (IAEA) in 1957. The IAEA's purpose is to promote and develop peaceful uses of nuclear energy to help people all over the world. Such energy can be used in health care, food production and for keeping the environment safe.

Nuclear power plants would soon be constructed that would provide a major source of electricity to citizens of the United States and other countries. Controversy would surround these plants with regard to their safety, high construction costs and storage of hazardous nuclear radioactive waste.

In health care, the IAEA's program of screening newborn babies for neo-natal hypothyroidism has been a success in Africa, Asia and Latin America. The disease causes mental retardation if undetected and untreated. The IAEA's radioimmunoassay technique has made possible for nations such as Thailand to screen all of its newborns using this low costing, safe (no radioactive exposure for patient) and relatively simple procedure. In 1999-2000 over 240 cases of congenital hypothyroidism were detected and treated in East and West Asia.[7]

In food production, radiation is used to develop more nutritional foods in countries such as the Philippines. There, radiation creates mutated breeds of rice plants that possess enhanced nutritional value. In other countries, radiation is used to eliminate pests that are harmful to livestock and crops. This is accomplished by sterilizing the insects with radiation, thus ending their reproduction capabilities. This method is environmentally safer than using pesticides to eliminate the insects.

In addition to promoting peaceful and productive uses of nuclear energy, the IAEA seeks to detect diversion for military purposes. The IAEA inspects nuclear facilities to ensure they are

---

[7] Source:International Atomic Energy Agency (www.iaea.org)

being used for peaceful pursuits in accordance with international treaties on non-proliferation of nuclear weapons. Only five nations are allowed to possess nuclear weapons facilities according to the Nuclear Non-Proliferation Treaty. These nations are the United States, Great Britain, Russia, China and France.

Dwight D. Eisenhower served as NATO's first Supreme Allied Commander prior to becoming the President of the United States. (NATO Photos)

Text of the address delivered by the President of the United States, Dwight D. Eisenhower, before the General Assembly of the United Nations in New York City, Tuesday afternoon, December 8, 1953.

Madame President, members of the General Assembly:

When Secretary General Hammarskjold's invitation to address this General Assembly reached me in Bermuda, I was just beginning a series of conferences with the Prime Ministers and Foreign Ministers of Great Britain and of France. Our subject was some of the problems that beset our world.

During the remainder of the Bermuda Conference, I had constantly in mind that ahead of me lay a great honor. That honor is mine today as I stand here, privileged to address the General Assembly of the United Nations.

At the same time that I appreciate the distinction of addressing you, I have a sense of exhilaration as I look upon this Assembly.

Never before in history has so much hope for so many people been gathered together in a single organization. Your deliberations and decisions during these somber years have already realized part of those hopes.

But the great test and the great accomplishments still lie ahead. And in the confident expectation of those accomplishments, I would use the office which, for the time being, I hold, to assure you that the Government of the United States will remain steadfast in its support of this body. This we shall do in the conviction that you will provide a great share of the wisdom, the courage, and the faith which can bring to this world lasting peace for all nations, and happiness and well-being for all men.

Clearly, it would not be fitting for me to take this occasion to present to you a unilateral American report on Bermuda. Nevertheless, I assure you that in our deliberations on that lovely island we sought to invoke those same great concepts of universal peace and human dignity which are so clearly etched in your Charter.

Neither would it be a measure of this great opportunity merely to recite, however hopefully, pious platitudes.

I therefore decided that this occasion warranted my saying to you some of the things that have been on the minds and hearts of my legislative and executive associates and on mine for a great many months--thoughts I had originally planned to say primarily to the American people.

I know that the American people share my deep belief that if a danger exists in the world, it is a danger shared by all – and equally, that if hope exists in the mind of one nation, that hope should be shared by all.

Finally, if there is to be advanced any proposal designed to ease even by the smallest measure the tensions of today's world, what more appropriate audience could there be than the members of the General Assembly of the United Nations?

I feel impelled to speak today in a language that in a sense is new – one which I, who has spent so much of my life in the military profession, would have preferred never to use.

That new language is the language of atomic warfare.

The atomic age has moved forward at such a pace that every citizen of the world should have some comprehension, at least in comparative terms, of the extent of this development of the utmost significance to every one of us. Clearly, if the people of the world are to conduct an intelligent search for peace, they must be armed with the significant facts of today's existence.

My recital of atomic danger and power is necessarily stated in United States terms, for these are the only incontrovertible facts that I know. I need hardly point out to this Assembly, however, that this subject is global, not merely national in character.

On July 16, 1945, the United States set off the world's first atomic explosion. Since that date in 1945, the United States of America has conducted 42 test explosions.

Atomic bombs today are more than 25 times as powerful as the weapons with which the atomic age dawned, while hydrogen weapons are in the ranges of millions of tons of TNT equivalent.

Today, the United States' stockpile of atomic weapons, which, of course, increases daily, exceeds by many times the explosive equivalent of the total of all bombs and all shells that came from every plane and every gun in every theatre of war in all of the years of World War II.

A single air group, whether afloat or land-based, can now deliver to any reachable target a destructive cargo exceeding in power all the bombs that fell on Britain in all of World War II.

In size and variety, the development of atomic weapons has been no less remarkable. The development has been such that atomic weapons have virtually achieved conventional status within our armed services. In the United States, the Army, the Navy, the Air Force, and the Marine Corps are all capable of putting this weapon to military use.

But the dread secret, and the fearful engines of atomic might, are not ours alone.

In the first place, the secret is possessed by our friends and allies, Great Britain and Canada, whose scientific genius made a tremendous contribution to our original discoveries, and the designs of atomic bombs.

The secret is also known by the Soviet Union.

The Soviet Union has informed us that, over recent years, it has devoted extensive resources to atomic weapons. During this period, the Soviet Union has exploded a series of atomic devices, including at least one involving thermo-nuclear reactions.

If at one time the United States possessed what might have been called a monopoly of atomic power, that monopoly ceased to exist several years ago. Therefore, although our earlier start has permitted us to accumulate what is today a great quantitative advantage, the atomic realities of today comprehend two facts of even greater significance.

First, the knowledge now possessed by several nations will eventually be shared by others—possibly all others.

Second, even a vast superiority in numbers of weapons, and a consequent capability of devastating retaliation, is no preventive, of itself, against the fearful material damage and toll of human lives that would be inflicted by surprise aggression.

The free world, at least dimly aware of these facts, has naturally embarked on a large program of warning and defense systems. That program will be accelerated and expanded.

But let no one think that the expenditure of vast sums for weapons and systems of defense can guarantee absolute safety for the cities and citizens of any nation. The awful arithmetic of the atomic bomb does not permit any such easy solution. Even against the most powerful defense, an aggressor in possession of the effective minimum number of atomic bombs for a surprise attack could probably place a sufficient number of his bombs on the chosen targets to cause hideous damage.

Should such an atomic attack be launched against the United States, our reactions would be swift and resolute. But for me to say that the defense capabilities of the United States are such that they could inflict terrible losses upon an aggressor – for me to say that the retaliation capabilities of the United States are so great that such an aggressor's land would be laid waste – all this, while fact, is not the true expression of the purpose and the hope of the United States.

To pause there would be to confirm the hopeless finality of a belief that two atomic colossi are doomed malevolently to eye each other indefinitely across a trembling world. To stop there would be to accept helplessly the probability of civilization destroyed – the annihilation of the irreplaceable heritage of mankind handed down to us generation from generation – and the condemnation of mankind to begin all over again the age-old struggle upward from savagery toward decency, and right, and justice.

Surely no sane member of the human race could discover victory in such desolation. Could anyone wish his name to be coupled by history with such human degradation and destruction.

Occasional pages of history do record the faces of the "Great Destroyers" but the whole book of history reveals mankind's never-ending quest for peace, and mankind's God-given capacity to build.

It is with the book of history, and not with isolated pages, that the United States will ever wish to be identified. My country wants to be constructive, not destructive. It wants agreement, not wars, among nations. It wants itself to live in freedom, and in the confidence that the people of every other nation enjoy equally the right of choosing their own way of life.

So my country's purpose is to help us move out of the dark chamber of horrors into the light, to find a way by which the minds of men, the hopes of men, the souls of men everywhere, can move forward toward peace and happiness and well being.

In this quest, I know that we must not lack patience. I know that in a world divided, such as ours today, salvation cannot be attained by one dramatic act.

I know that many steps will have to be taken over many months before the world can look at itself one day and truly realize that a new climate of mutually peaceful confidence is abroad in the world.

But I know, above all else, that we must start to take these steps – now.

The United States and its allies, Great Britain and France, have over the past months tried to take some of these steps. Let no one say that we shun the conference table.

On the record has long stood the request of the United States, Great Britain and France to negotiate with the Soviet Union the problems of a divided Germany.

On the record has long stood the request of the same three nations to negotiate the problems of Korea.

Most recently, we have received from the Soviet Union what is in effect an expression of willingness to hold a Four Power meeting. Along with our allies, Great Britain and France, we were pleased to see that this note did not contain the unacceptable preconditions previously put forward.

As you already know from our joint Bermuda communiqué, the United States, Great Britain, and France have agreed promptly to meet with the Soviet Union.

The Government of the United States approaches this conference with hopeful sincerity. We will bend every effort of our minds to the single purpose of emerging from that conference with tangible results toward peace – the only true way of lessening international tension.

We never have, we never will, propose or suggest that the Soviet Union surrender what is rightfully theirs.

We will never say that the people of Russia are an enemy with whom we have no desire ever to deal or mingle in friendly and fruitful relationship.

On the contrary, we hope that this coming Conference may initiate a relationship with the Soviet Union which will eventually bring about a free intermingling of the peoples of the east and of the west – the one sure, human way of developing the understanding required for confident and peaceful relations.

Instead of the discontent which is now settling upon Eastern Germany, occupied Austria, and countries of Eastern Europe, we seek a harmonious family of free European nations, with none a threat to the other, and least of all a threat to the peoples of Russia.

Beyond the turmoil and strife and misery of Asia, we seek peaceful opportunity for these peoples to develop their natural resources and to elevate their lives.

These are not idle works or shallow visions. Behind them lies a story of nations lately come to independence, not as a result of war, but through free grant or peaceful negotiation. There is a record, already written, of assistance gladly given by nations of the west to needy peoples, and to those suffering the temporary effects of famine, drought, and natural disaster.

These are deeds of peace. They speak more loudly than promises or protestations of peaceful intent.

But I do not wish to rest either upon the reiteration of past proposals or the restatement of past deeds. The gravity of the time is such that every new avenue of peace, no matter how dimly discernible, should be explored.

There is at least one new avenue of peace which has not yet been well explored – an avenue now laid out by the General Assembly of the United Nations.

In its resolution of November 18th, 1953 this General Assembly suggested – and I quote – "that the Disarmament Commission study the desirability of establishing a sub-committee consisting of representatives of the Powers principally involved, which should seek in private an acceptable solution... and report on such a solution to the General Assembly and to the Security Council not later than 1 September 1954."

The United States, heeding the suggestion of the General Assembly of the United Nations, is instantly prepared to meet privately with such other countries as may be "principally involved," to seek "an acceptable solution" to the atomic armaments race which overshadows not only the peace, but the very life, of the world.

We shall carry into these private or diplomatic talks a new conception.

The United States would seek more than the mere reduction or elimination of atomic materials for military purposes.

It is not enough to take this weapon out of the hands of the soldiers. It must be put in the hands of those who will know how to strip its military casing and adapt it to the arts of peace.

The United States knows that if the fearful trend of atomic military build up can be reversed, the greatest of destructive forces can be developed into a great boon, for the benefit of all mankind.

The United States knows that peaceful power from atomic energy is no dream of the future. That capability, already proved, is here--now-- today. Who can doubt, if the entire body of the world's scientists and engineers had adequate amounts of fissionable material with which to test and develop their ideas, that this capability would rapidly be transformed into universal, efficient, and economic usage.

To hasten the day when fear of the atom will begin to disappear from the minds of people, and the governments of the East and West, there are certain steps that can be taken now.

I therefore make the following proposals:

The Governments principally involved, to the extent permitted by elementary prudence, to begin now and continue to make joint contributions from their stockpiles of normal uranium and fissionable materials to an international Atomic Energy Agency. We would expect that such an agency would be set up under the aegis of the United Nations.

The ratios of contributions, the procedures and other details would properly be within the scope of the "private conversations" I have referred to earlier.

The United States is prepared to undertake these explorations in good faith. Any partner of the United States acting in the same good faith will find the United States a not unreasonable or ungenerous associate.

Undoubtedly initial and early contributions to this plan would be small in quantity. However, the proposal has the great virtue that it can be undertaken without the irritations and mutual suspicions incident to any attempt to set up a completely acceptable system of world-wide inspection and control.

The Atomic Energy Agency could be made responsible for the impounding, storage, and protection of the contributed fissionable and other materials. The ingenuity of our scientists will provide special safe conditions under which such a bank of fissionable material can be made essentially immune to surprise seizure.

The more important responsibility of this Atomic Energy Agency would be to devise methods whereby this fissionable material would be allocated to serve the peaceful pursuits of mankind. Experts would be mobilized to apply atomic energy to the needs of agriculture, medicine, and other peaceful activities. A special purpose would be to provide abundant electrical energy in the power-starved areas of the world. Thus the contributing powers would be dedicating some of their strength to serve the needs rather than the fears of mankind.

The United States would be more than willing – it would be proud to take up with others "principally involved" the development of plans whereby such peaceful use of atomic energy would be expedited.

Of those "principally involved" the Soviet Union must, of course, be one.

I would be prepared to submit to the Congress of the United States, and with every expectation of approval, any such plan that would:

First – encourage world-wide investigation into the most effective peace time uses of fissionable material, and with the certainty that they had all the material needed for the conduct of all experiments that were appropriate;

Second – begin to diminish the potential destructive power of the world's atomic stockpiles;

Third – allow all peoples of all nations to see that, in this enlightened age, the great powers of the earth, both of the East and of the West, are interested in human aspirations first, rather than in building up the armaments of war;

Fourth – open up a new channel for peaceful discussion, and initiate at least a new approach to the many difficult problems that must be solved in both private and public conversations, if the world is to shake off the inertia imposed by fear, and is to make positive progress toward peace.

Against the dark background of the atomic bomb, the United States does not wish merely to present strength, but also the desire and the hope for peace.

The coming months will be fraught with fateful decisions. In this Assembly; in the capitals and military headquarters of the world; in the hearts of men everywhere, be they governors, or governed, may they be decisions which will lead this work out of fear and into peace.

To the making of these fateful decisions, the United States pledges before you – and therefore before the world – its determination to help solve the fearful atomic dilemma – to devote its entire heart and mind to find the way by which the miraculous inventiveness of man shall not be dedicated to his death, but consecrated to his life.

I again thank the delegates for the great honor they have done me, in inviting me to appear before them, and in listening to me so courteously. Thank you.

Headquarters of the International Atomic Energy Agency in 1968 (IAEA)

The first IAEA preliminary assistance mission is shown on its return from Latin America in 1958. The purpose of the mission was to do research for establishing training centers for the peaceful applications of atomic energy. (IAEA)

Water samples from Member States are being prepared for analysis at the IAEA's Isotope Hydrology lab in Vienna, Austria (Pavlicek/IAEA)

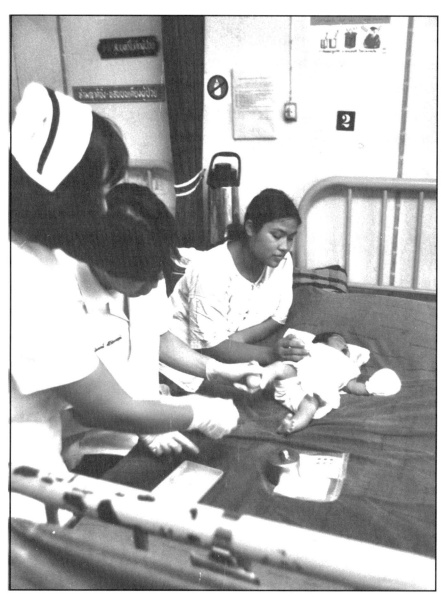

IAEA project on neo-natal hypothyroidism (children's brain research) at Surat Thani Hospital in southern Thailand (H.F./IAEA)

The IAEA assists Member States in improving nutritional quality of plants through radiation-induced mutation breeding. Here, a rice paddy in the Philippines. (D. Kindley/IAEA)

7th UN inspection in Iraq. Damaged Tammuz-2 reactor at Tuwaitha, Iraq (Mouchkin/IAEA)

While the accomplishments of the IAEA have been many, there have been some failures. For instance, the IAEA was unable to detect the nuclear weapons program in Iraq prior to the Gulf War of 1991.[8] Under the Nuclear Non-Proliferation Treaty, Iraq was prohibited from developing such weapons. Issues such as these inspections would have to be addressed. Regardless of such failures, the IAEA has had a positive impact on the world since its inception in 1957. The peaceful applications of nuclear energy are improving the quality of life in almost every part of the world on a daily basis.

---

[8] The Gulf War was fought as a result of Iraq's invasion of neighboring Kuwait in 1990. An allied coalition, led by the United States launched a massive air and ground campaign in early 1991 to expel the Iraqi army from Kuwait. Within several months the mission was accomplished and Kuwait was liberated.

Chapter Four
Nuclear Weapons and the Public

"New thermonuclear weapons are tremendously powerful; however, they are not, in many ways, as powerful as is world opinion...."[9]

These words ring true. During the 1950's and 1960's public outcry towards the hundreds of nuclear test explosions by the Soviet Union and the U.S. was immense. The public had much to fear. The destructive effects of an atomic bomb were clearly demonstrated by the attacks on Hiroshima and Nagasaki. Throughout the 1950's, development and testing of nuclear weapons continued by the United States, the Soviet Union and Great Britain. These tests were conducted for a variety of reasons including to simulate the effects of blasts on civilian life and various building structures, and to improve the power of the nuclear arsenal. Other tests were carried out in conjunction with military exercises to understand the capabilities of soldiers in nuclear warfare. Many of the United States nuclear tests were conducted within its own borders, at the Nevada Test Site.

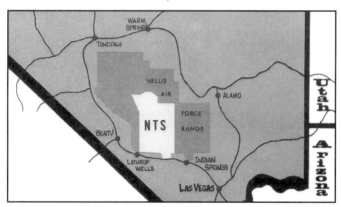

Map of the Nevada Test Site (U.S. Department of Energy photograph)

---

[9]Memorandum of Conference with the President, August 14, 1958, see page 126

Shed beside liquid petroleum tank, both smoldering from heat of flash from the U.S. nuclear test-Operation Cue in Nevada (National Archives)

Shed disintegrates as blast wave hits in Operation Cue (National Archives)

A number of these nuclear tests were atmospheric explosions. The resulting fallout from those tests, both radioactive and political, garnered world opinion to demand a cessation of nuclear testing. Fears of a nuclear war and radioactive fallout were addressed by the Federal Civil Defense Administration.[10] Nevertheless, anxiety over nuclear testing and the arms race would grip the public. There was a strong call for action! Public opinion clearly influenced President Dwight D. Eisenhower's decision making.

"I had come to the conclusion that, in view of worldwide apprehensions, we should propose a ban, strictly limited as to time, on the testing of nuclear weapons."[11]

Banning nuclear test explosions was at least one measure employed to slow down the escalating nuclear arms race. It could also prevent further radioactive fallout. President Eisenhower's public statement of August 22, 1958 expressed hope that a nuclear test suspension could lead to further disarmament agreements.[12] A brief suspension of nuclear testing would come about in the late 1950's. However, full-scale testing would resume in the 1960's and with it, the nuclear arsenals of both the Soviet Union and the U.S. would grow more powerful.

The public's anxiety over fallout was clearly justified. Later studies would substantiate those fears. In 2001, a preliminary report released by the Centers for Disease Control stated that every American living in the United States after 1951 was exposed to radioactive fallout from nuclear tests worldwide. At least 11,000 deaths were estimated to have been caused by cancer resulting from external exposure to fallout.[13] The study also cited exposures worldwide, noting that "A number of populations outside the

---

[10] For an example of this see page 145

[11] Eisenhower, Dwight D., "Waging Peace," Doubleday Publishing, p. 476

[12] For full text of statement see page 128

[13] Progress Report on the Feasibility Study of the Health Consequences to the American Population of Nuclear Weapons Tests Conducted by the United States and Other Nations, August 2001 (www.cdc.gov)

United States have been exposed to higher levels of radioiodine and other radionuclides than the United States population. These populations include the residents of the Marshall Islands;[14] people living near the nuclear weapons site in Semipalantinsk, Kazakhstan;[15] people exposed to large releases from the Chernobyl nuclear power station accident in Ukraine and people living near the Mayak nuclear fuel reprocessing plant in Russia."[16]

New Zealand's Minister of Foreign Affairs, Phil Goff, commented on the U.S. nuclear testing in the Pacific Ocean during the 1950's and its effects:

> *"The early tests of Maralinga and Montebello, the Marshall Islands and Christmas Islands were conducted in the atmosphere with little attention to their impact on the environment, the people displaced by them or indeed those who observed them."[17]*

Radioactive fallout was one of the greatest fears for people worldwide and its effects are still being felt today. But by far the greatest fear for the public was a nuclear confrontation. And one fall day in 1962 that nightmare was becoming a reality.....

---

[14] The Marshall Islands are located in the Pacific Ocean and an area where scores of U.S. nuclear tests were conducted in the 1950's.

[15] Inside the former Soviet Union where a number of nuclear tests were conducted.

[16] A feasibility report.... See footnote 11

[17] Statement by the Hon. Phil Goff at the Conference on Facilitating the Entry into Force of the Comprehensive Nuclear Test Ban Treaty, November 11, 2001

OVER 2,000 NUCLEAR TEST EXPLOSIONS HAVE BEEN CONDUCTED SINCE 1945. (PHOTO COURTESY NATIONAL ARCHIVES)

NUCLEAR TESTS BY NATION:

United States	1,054	China	45
Soviet Union	715	India	3
France	210	Pakistan	2
Great Britain	45		

Note: There have been 24 joint U.S.-U.K. tests.

Chapter Five
The Cuban Missile Crisis and the Limited Test Ban Treaty

United States aerial photographs revealed the unthinkable. The Soviets had placed nuclear missiles in Cuba, well within striking distance of American cities.

This aerial photograph shows part of the nuclear missile buildup by the Soviet Union in Cuba, just south of the United States. IRBM Launch Site No. 1 in Guanajay, Cuba on October 23, 1962 (JFK Library)

The United States responded by placing a naval quarantine around Cuba to prevent further weapons buildup, and critical negotiations ensued between U.S. president John F. Kennedy and Soviet premier Nikita Khrushchev. The situation was resolved with the U.S pledging not to attack the Soviet's ally, Cuba. The Soviet missiles were to be dismantled and removed. The crisis may have been averted, but the fear of nuclear war lingered.

The following is the text of a statement of the President, John F. Kennedy, on November 2, 1962 in regard to the Cuban Missile Crisis.

My fellow citizens: I want to take this opportunity to report on the conclusions which this Government has reached on the basis of yesterday's aerial photographs which will be made available tomorrow, as well as other indications, namely, that the Soviet missile bases in Cuba are being dismantled, their missiles and related equipment are being crated, and the fixed installations at these sites are being destroyed.

The United States intends to follow closely the completion of this work through a variety of means, including aerial surveillance, until such time as an equally satisfactory international means of verification is effected.

While the quarantine remains in effect, we are hopeful that adequate procedures can be developed for international inspection of Cuba-bound cargoes. The International Committee of the Red Cross, in our view, would be an appropriate agent in this matter.

The continuation of these measures in air and sea, until the threat to peace posed by these offensive weapons is gone, is in keeping with our pledge to secure their withdrawal or elimination from this Hemisphere. It is in keeping with the resolution of the OAS, and it is in keeping with the exchange of letters with Chairman Khrushchev of October 27th and 28th.

Progress is now being made towards the restoration of peace in the Caribbean, and it is our firm hope and purpose that this progress shall go forward. We will continue to keep the American people informed on this vital matter.

Thank you.

"This treaty is not the millennium. It will not resolve all conflicts, or cause the Communists to forego their ambitions, or eliminate the dangers of war. It will not reduce our need for arms or allies or programs of assistance to others. But it is an important first step – a step towards peace – a step towards reason – a step away from war."

These are the words of John F. Kennedy as he addressed the nation regarding the Limited Test Ban Treaty signed with the Soviet Union and the United Kingdom in 1963. This agreement came almost on the heels of the Cuban Missile Crisis. It wasn't the desired comprehensive nuclear test ban that both President Eisenhower and President Kennedy had hoped to achieve. Nor, as JFK noted in his speech, was it the end to the nuclear arms race. However, it was a step in the right direction. The treaty banned all nuclear weapons tests or any other nuclear explosions in the atmosphere, underwater and outer space. Underground nuclear tests would be allowed to continue under the agreement, provided radioactive fallout from the explosion did not leave the territory of the testing nation. The dangers to the environment as a result of continued nuclear testing were a significant concern worldwide. Limitations on the size of those underground tests would come with the Threshold Test Ban Treaty signed between the Soviet Union and the United States in 1974.

Despite the signing of the Limited Test Ban Treaty, more nuclear tests were conducted in the 1960's than any other decade. Many of those tests were carried out before the treaty, but hundreds afterwards as well. However, the 1970's overall saw a tremendous reduction in nuclear weapons testing by both the U.S. and the Soviet Union and this trend continued into the 1980's. In the 1990's the total number of nuclear tests dipped under twenty, as opposed to the over 600 test explosions during the 1960's. The Limited Test Ban Treaty was a significant achievement towards ending the nuclear weapons nightmare.

In his speech, President Kennedy reflected on the reality of a nuclear holocaust.

> "*A war today or tomorrow, if it led to nuclear war, would not be like any war in history. A full-scale nuclear exchange, lasting less than 60 minutes, with the weapons now in existence, could wipe out more than 300 million Americans, Europeans and Russians, as well as untold numbers elsewhere. And the survivors, as Chairman Khrushchev warned the Communist Chinese, 'The survivors would envy the dead.' For they would inherit a world so devastated by explosions and poison and fire that today we cannot even conceive of its horrors. So let us try to turn the world from war. Let us make the most of this opportunity, and every opportunity, to reduce tension, to slow down the perilous nuclear arms race, and to check the world's slide toward final annihilation.*"

Signing of the Limited Test Ban Treaty in 1963 (JFK Library)

The coming years would see further efforts to reduce nuclear weapons proliferation and testing. President Kennedy looked ahead to these efforts, although he would not be able to see them come to fruition. These efforts would culminate in the Nuclear Non-Proliferation Treaty whose aim was to prevent more nations from gaining weapons of mass destruction.

"I ask you to stop and think for a moment what it would mean to have nuclear weapons in so many hands, in the hands of countries large and small, stable and unstable, responsible and irresponsible, scattered throughout the world. There would be no rest for anyone then, no stability, no real security, and no chance of effective disarmament. There would be only the increased chance of accidental war, and an increased necessity for the great powers to involve themselves in what otherwise would be local conflicts."

"He (Under-Secretary Harriman) also made clear our strong preference for a more comprehensive treaty banning all tests everywhere, and our ultimate goal for general and complete disarmament."

John F. Kennedy

Efforts to enter into force the Comprehensive Test Ban Treaty were stalled as of the year 2001. This treaty would ban all nuclear test explosions. The United States was among the nations who did not ratify the Comprehensive Test Ban Treaty.

Chapter Six
Nuclear Weapons Today

By the late 1960's the nuclear weapons race was not solely about the Soviet Union and the United States. France, China and Great Britain all had nuclear weapons capability by the year 1968. It was thought quite likely that other nations would soon join them.

In 1968 the majority of nations signed the Nuclear Non-Proliferation Treaty. The United States, Soviet Union, China, Great Britain and France agreed not to aid any non-nuclear weapons nation in developing such weapons. In addition, these five countries, officially established as the five nuclear weapons nations, were to work towards nuclear disarmament. All other nations signing the treaty were prohibited from developing nuclear weapons and agreed to submit to inspections of their nuclear facilities by the IAEA. These inspections were to certify that these facilities were being used only for peaceful purposes.

India and Pakistan are among the few nations who did not join the Non-Proliferation Treaty as of the year 2001. While embroiled in a bloody struggle for control of the Kashmir Region, these bordering nations have each developed and tested nuclear weapons. They have fought three wars since 1947 and are constantly on the brink of another, particularly when it comes to the issue of Kashmir. Both India and Pakistan claim the area as their own and consequently, Kashmir is divided between them. The "Line of Control" separates India's and Pakistan's portion of Kashmir. Troops are a fixture at the Line of Control where gunshots and artillery fire are frequently exchanged. It is in a regional conflict such as this that the danger of nuclear warfare now lies.

Site of the 1974 nuclear test conducted by India (AP/ Wide World photos)

Indian army preparing to shell Pakistani positions in Kashmir during fighting in 1998 (AP/Wide World photos)

"Nonetheless, unresolved disagreements, deep animosity and distrust, and the continuing confrontation between their forces in disputed Kashmir make the subcontinent a region with a significant risk of nuclear confrontation."[18]

In addition to tensions with Pakistan, India has had a history of conflict with another nuclear weapons neighbor, China. In 1962 India was defeated by China in a border war. In 1964 China conducted its first nuclear test explosion. The escalating tension caused by China's nuclear weapons program and testing in the 1960's hastened India to develop its own nuclear bomb. Following China's third nuclear test explosion in 1966, Indian opinion was mixed. However,

"A number of influential Calcutta dailies (newspapers) came out strongly for bomb manufacture. This also held true for New Delhi's Urdu dailies. In Madras, opinion was mixed, but Andhra Prabha felt that 'undoubtedly, nuclear weapons production by India is the only alternative' to the present situation."[19]

Another Indian journal was quoted as saying that Communist China's A-bomb blast 'will set off a chain reaction' of nuclear bomb development that may 'shove all this disarmament talk down the drain.'[20] This assessment was accurate as India detonated its first nuclear bomb eight years later in 1974. Pakistan was to follow suit thereafter and now today, three neighboring nations in Asia possess nuclear weaponry. The situation in Asia illustrates the negative impact of nuclear weapons development and testing. Both Pakistan and India have yet to sign the

---

[18] Office of the Secretary of Defense, "Proliferation: Threat and Response," November 1997, p.20.

[19] United States Information Agency, "Worldwide Reaction to Communist China's Third Nuclear Explosion" (May 12, 1966), Courtesy National Archives. See Appendix, p. 154

[20] Ibid

Comprehensive Test Ban Treaty as of the year 2001. They have each conducted tests as recently as 1998. China has signed, but not ratified, the Comprehensive Test Ban Treaty as of March 2001.

There has also been a history of conflict on the Korean peninsula. War raged between North and South Korea from 1950-53. The United States came to the aid of South Korea and heavily engaged the North Korean army. The fighting ceased with a truce in 1953 and the two nations were separated along the 38th parallel. U.S. troops have been stationed in South Korea ever since the 1953 truce. North Korea is a nation who signed and ratified the Non-Proliferation Treaty, but in 1993 denied IAEA inspectors access to facilities that were suspected of harboring nuclear weapons development. Once again, tensions began to run high on the Korean peninsula. With the possible advent of nuclear weapons on the peninsula, there could be no hope for peace. In 1994 an agreement between the United States and North Korea called for the closure of the suspect facilities in exchange for two new nuclear reactors to be constructed by South Korea. These reactors would be less conducive to diverting materials into weapons of mass destruction. In 2000 a historic summit meeting occurred between the leaders of the North and the South, bringing hopes of possible reunification.

In the Middle East, Iraq has refused to allow thorough inspections of its nuclear facilities by the IAEA since 1998. Prior to the Gulf War of 1991, Iraq's development of nuclear weapons went undetected by the IAEA's inspectors. As of 2001, the status of Iraq's nuclear weapons program was unclear and the IAEA is still barred from completing full-scale inspections. According to a report from the U.S. Office of the Secretary of Defense, "Iraq's nuclear weapons program suffered a very significant setback from the Gulf War bombing of nuclear-related facilities.......but considerable expertise (scientists and technicians) and possibly some documentation and infrastructure, survived."[21]

By the late 1980's, the Soviet Union was crumbling and the Cold War was about to come to an end. Both the Soviet Union and the United States had tens of thousands of nuclear weapons,

---

[21] Office of the Secretary of Defense, "Proliferation: Threat and Response," November 1997, p. 31

and it was an exhausting arms race economically for each to sustain. The two nations signed the Intermediate Range Nuclear Forces (INF) Treaty in 1987, which eliminated intermediate and shorter range nuclear missiles on both sides. No longer was there an emphasis on building more powerful weapons. Other priorities would emerge in the 1990's, including the security and safety of nuclear weapons materials in the former Soviet Union. Former Soviet states, such as the Ukraine and Belarus, had gained independence but had also inherited nuclear weapons. With the harsh economic conditions facing Russia and the former republics, financial assistance would be needed to ensure the safety and security of nuclear weapons related material. The United States Cooperative Threat Reduction Program has been instrumental in assisting Russia and the former Soviet republics in the safe storage, transportation and dismantling of nuclear weapons related material. Nuclear weapons from the former republics were safely transferred to Russia or dismantled.

Russia still possessed a massive nuclear arms stockpile at the end of the Cold War. Strategic Arms Reduction talks with the United States have produced two treaties (START I and START II) which aim to have nuclear warheads reduced to 3,000-3,500 on each side by the year 2007. By the end of the 20th century, the chance of a nuclear holocaust between the U.S. and Russia had been greatly reduced. Other challenges lay ahead at the dawn of the new century, not involving the building of nuclear weapons but defense against them. The United States has announced its plans to build a national missile defense system. However, such a system violates the 1972 Anti-Ballistic Missile (ABM) Treaty with the Soviet Union that prohibits ballistic missile defense. The latest U.S. proposal of missile defense is not intended to prevent an onslaught from an arsenal the size of Russia's. The United States missile defense is targeted for defending against attacks from smaller nations that could obtain several nuclear weapons. By the end of 2001 the United States, against Russia's wishes, had announced its intention to unilaterally withdraw from the ABM Treaty. For some, this provoked fears of a new nuclear arms race. Nations such as Russia or China could augment their nuclear stockpiles to ensure their capability of overwhelming the U.S. missile defense system. Instead, the U.S. and Russia were discussing further cuts in their nuclear weapons arsenals, beyond what is required by START I and II. A treaty reducing the number of nuclear weapons for both the United States and Russia was signed on May 24, 2002. (see page 169)

U.S. President George W. Bush and Russian President Vladimar Putin at the White House in November 2001. Among the items on their summit agenda: Nuclear weapons reductions. (AP/ Wide World Photo)

National Missile Defense Test

A payload launch vehicle carrying a prototype interceptor is launched from Kwajalein Missile Range for a planned intercept of a ballistic missile target. This particular test was unsuccessful. The test was conducted on Jan. 18, 2000.   Another test conducted in July 2001 was successful. (Department of Defense)

THE WHITE HOUSE

90041

WASHINGTON

November 16, 1981

NATIONAL SECURITY DECISION
DIRECTIVE NUMBER 15

THEATER NUCLEAR FORCES
(Intermediate-Range Nuclear Forces)

On the recommendation of the National Security Council, which met on November 12, 1981, I have made the following decisions regarding the U.S. position for the first round of the negotiations on Intermediate-Range Nuclear Forces (INF) scheduled to begin on November 30, 1981.

-- We will propose an agreement on intermediate-range land-based systems that would remove and dismantle the Soviet Union's SS-20 and retire SS-4 and SS-5 systems in return for no deployment of the U.S. Pershing II and GLCMs.

-- We will also indicate that we are prepared to seek subsequent limits with signficant reductions for other nuclear weapons systems.

-- We will negotiate in good faith to achieve global, equal and verifiable levels of weapons.

-- The Interagency Group will ensure that the negotiating instructions, including enumeration of objectives and principles, are fully congruent with the President's decisions as expressed in this National Security Decision Directive.

Ronald Reagan

Review on November 12, 2001
Extended by R. V. Allen
Reason: NSC 1.13 (c) (e)
Declassify on: OADR

Declassified/Released on 5-17-91
under provisions of E.O. 12356
by S. Tilley, National Security Council

(F87-1035)

Intermediate range nuclear forces negotiations (Ronald Reagan Library)

57

President Reagan and General Secretary Mikhail Gorbachev signing the INF Treaty in the White House (Ronald Reagan Library)

Chapter Seven
The Comprehensive Test Ban Treaty

Both President Eisenhower and President Kennedy realized that a nuclear test ban treaty was not, by itself, going to halt nuclear proliferation. However, they understood a test ban's significance toward achieving that end. Their negotiations produced the Limited Test Ban Treaty with the Soviet Union in 1963 (see pages 47-49), thereby slowing down the momentum of destruction exhibited by the two rivals. Underground nuclear testing would continue though.

In 1996 the United Nations General Assembly voted overwhelmingly to adopt the Comprehensive Test Ban Treaty (CTBT). This treaty would completely ban nuclear weapons test explosions or other nuclear explosions. In order for the treaty to take effect, forty-four nations with a nuclear capacity must join. As of 2001, thirty-one of those forty-four nations have ratified the treaty, including three major nuclear powers, Great Britain, France and Russia.

At a United Nations conference on November 11, 2001 foreign ministers from around the world called for ratification of the CTBT. New Zealand's Phil Goff noted the tensions of nuclear neighbors, India and Pakistan. "Nuclear capabilities on the Indian subcontinent together with tensions in the region make it the most dangerous place in the world. It is in the interests of both states to sign the Treaty to reduce the risks." Great Britain's Jack Straw stated, "….the cessation of all nuclear explosions will constitute an effective measure of nuclear disarmament and non-proliferation."

The United States signed the Comprehensive Test Ban Treaty in 1996. However, the Senate rejected ratification in 1999, claiming it was not verifiable. They feared other nations could "cheat" and carry on undetected nuclear weapons test explosions despite international monitoring. In addition, many senators believed the U.S. nuclear stockpile could not be maintained without actual nuclear test explosions. The issue of verification is critical for a treaty of this type, and has been so since negotiations started on a test ban treaty in the 1950's.

The CTBT features an international monitoring system (IMS) to detect nuclear explosions. Over 300 facilities make up this system, which uses a variety of methods to detect nuclear explosions. These include seismic, hydroacoustic, infrasound, and radionuclide stations and laboratories located all over the world. These stations are equipped to detect nuclear explosions underground, underwater or in the atmosphere.

Can a nation "cheat" and carry out a nuclear explosion undetected via some evasive method? Former Chairman of the Joint Chiefs of Staff, General John Shalikashvili touches upon this issue in his report, titled "Findings and Recommendations Concerning the CTBT."

> "...it is not so easy to advance a nuclear weapons program through evasive testing as some people fear. A potential cheater would have to calculate correctly the combined capabilities of national, international and scientific monitoring systems."[22]

An independent commission on the verifiability of the CTBT studied the possibility of a nation attempting to evade the IMS and conduct a nuclear test explosion. Their report discussed the evasion tactic called *decoupling*, a technique to disguise a nuclear explosion underground. The report's conclusion was...

> "In theory, decoupling would work by conducting a test in a large underground cavity in an attempt to attenuate greatly the seismic waves. A large enough cavity at a sufficient depth would have to be found or constructed to permit such an attempt. Successful decoupling would require substantial financial, technical and human resources and would need to be conducted in complete secrecy."[23]

---

[22] Shalikashvili, General John M., "Findings and Recommendations Concerning the Comprehensive Nuclear Test Ban Treaty."

[23] Independent Commission on the Verifiability of the CTBT: Final Report, November 7, 2000 p. 8

The report goes on to conclude that......

> *"These global capabilities (the international monitoring system) constitute a complex and constantly evolving verification gauntlet, which any potential violator will have to confront--together they will serve as a powerful deterrent."*[24]

In other words, it would be difficult and risky for a nation to "cheat" and carry out a nuclear explosion under the CTBT. Without question, the possibility of evading the IMS is of serious concern. And it has been for some time. Dr. James Killian, scientific advisor to President Eisenhower, wrote about this issue over forty years ago during negotiations for a nuclear test ban.

> *"In a world of rapidly changing technology, it may be impossible to devise foolproof monitoring systems—either for nuclear test cessation or for other forms of agreed limitations. The most that these systems may accomplish will be to make evasion very costly and very uncertain. These may be the principal functions of monitoring systems."*[25]

Dr. Killian goes on to point out that the effectiveness of an international monitoring system can be augmented.

> *"Hence, if they (international monitoring system) are to be of maximum use to us, they would have to be supplemented by highly-developed intelligence systems of our own and with appropriate military measures."*[26]

---

[24] Ibid, p. 8

[25] Killian, Jr., J.R. "Memorandum On Some Technical Factors Involved in Policy Decisions On Arms Limitations and Specifically on the Limitation of Nuclear Testing." 3/30/1959, p.6 (Dwight D. Eisenhower Library) See page 129

[26] Ibid

General Shalikashvili makes the same point in his report nearly forty years later.

> "Once the Test Ban Treaty enters into force, the United States will use its own intelligence assets and additional capabilities provided under the Treaty to verify compliance with it."[27]

He also talks about the valuable information the United States currently receives from the treaty's international monitoring system. The national security of the U.S. would only be enhanced by a fully operational IMS once the treaty enters into force.

> "The United States already receives valuable data from the IMS. For example, seismic stations in the partially completed (IMS) system picked up signals from several recent 100-ton chemical explosions at the former Soviet test site in Kazakhstan….. The full IMS…..will provide global coverage that vastly surpasses the monitoring capabilities that the United States relied on during the Cold War."[28]

One can also safely assume that the ability to detect nuclear explosions will improve over time, as is the case with almost any technology. So too could evasive techniques, and it could forever be a game of cat and mouse.

General Shalikashvili's report also reviews the maintenance of nuclear weapons under a test ban treaty. The term for maintaining nuclear weapons without test explosions is referred to as Stockpile Stewardship.

> "Almost all of the approximately 4,000--6,000 parts of a nuclear weapon, including all safety- and reliability-critical electrical, mechanical, and alarming

---

[27] Shalikashvili, General John M., Findings and Recommendations Concerning the CTBT

[28] Ibid

subsystems, are outside of the "physics package," – i.e. the subsystem that creates the nuclear explosion. Under the Test Ban Treaty, these parts can still be thoroughly tested, …..The SSP (Stockpile Stewardship Program) also has the world's most powerful computers. They are offering an increasingly sophisticated capability to model potential changes in warhead performance by analyzing data from new experiments that do not involve nuclear explosions in conjunction with data from historical tests of existing weapon designs."[29]

It should be noted that the treaty allows for a nation to withdraw should "extraordinary events" (Article IX) dictate such action.

The Comprehensive Test Ban Treaty

Preamble

The States Parties to this Treaty (hereinafter referred to as "the States Parties"),

Welcoming the international agreements and other positive measures of recent years in the field of nuclear disarmament, including reductions in arsenals of nuclear weapons, as well as in the field of the prevention of nuclear proliferation in all its aspects,

Underlining the importance of the full and prompt implementation of such agreements and measures,

Convinced that the present international situation provides an opportunity to take further effective measures towards nuclear disarmament and against the proliferation of nuclear weapons in

---

[29] Findings and Recommendations Concerning the Comprehensive Nuclear Test Ban Treaty, by General John Shalikashvili

all its aspects, and declaring their intention to take such measures,

Stressing therefore the need for continued systematic and progressive efforts to reduce nuclear weapons globally, with the ultimate goal of eliminating those weapons, and of general and complete disarmament under strict and effective international control,

Recognizing that the cessation of all nuclear weapon test explosions and all other nuclear explosions, by constraining the development and qualitative improvement of nuclear weapons and ending the development of advanced new types of nuclear weapons, constitutes an effective measure of nuclear disarmament and non-proliferation in all its aspects,

Further recognizing that an end to all such nuclear explosions will thus constitute a meaningful step in the realization of a systematic process to achieve nuclear disarmament,

Convinced that the most effective way to achieve an end to nuclear testing is through the conclusion of a universal and internationally and effectively verifiable comprehensive nuclear test-ban treaty, which has long been one of the highest priority objectives of the international community in the field of disarmament and non-proliferation,

Noting the aspirations expressed by the Parties to the 1963 Treaty Banning Nuclear Weapons Tests in the Atmosphere, in Outer Space and Under Water to seek to achieve the discontinuance of all test explosions of nuclear weapons for all time,

Noting also the views expressed that this treaty could contribute to the protection of the environment,

Affirming the purpose of attracting the adherence of all States to this Treaty and its objective to contribute effectively to the prevention of the proliferation of nuclear weapons in all its aspects, to the process of nuclear disarmament and therefore to the enhancement of international peace and security,

Have agreed as follows:

Article I of the treaty:
1. Each State Party undertakes not to carry out any nuclear weapon test explosion or any other nuclear explosion, and to prohibit and prevent any such nuclear explosion at any place under its jurisdiction or control.

2. Each State party undertakes, furthermore, to refrain from causing, encouraging, or in any way participating in the carrying out of any nuclear weapon test explosion or any other nuclear explosion.

The treaty goes on to detail key provisions such as an international monitoring system to detect nuclear test explosions and items such as duration and withdrawal.

44 nations which are required to sign and ratify the CTBT:

Country	Signed Treaty	Ratified Treaty
Algeria	October 15, 1996	
Argentina	September 24, 1996	December 4, 1998
Australia	September 24, 1996	July 9, 1998
Austria	September 24, 1996	March 13, 1998
Bangladesh	October 24, 1996	March 8, 2000
Belgium	September 24, 1996	June 29, 1999
Brazil	September 24, 1996	July 24, 1998
Bulgaria	September 24, 1996	September 29, 1999
Canada	September 24, 1996	December 18, 1998
Chile	September 24, 1996	July 12, 2000
China	September 24, 1996	
Colombia	September 24, 1996	
D.P.R. of Korea		
D.P.R. of the Congo	October 4, 1996	
Egypt	October 14, 1996	
Finland	September 24, 1996	January 15, 1999
France	September 24, 1996	April 6, 1998
Germany	September 24, 1996	August 20, 1998
Hungary	September 25, 1996	July 13, 1999
India		
Indonesia	September 24, 1996	
Iran	September 24, 1996	
Israel	September 25, 1996	
Italy	September 24, 1996	February 1, 1999
Japan	September 24, 1996	July 8, 1997
Mexico	September 24, 1996	October 5, 1999
Netherlands	September 24, 1996	March 23, 1999
Norway	September 24, 1996	July 15, 1999
Pakistan		
Peru	September 25, 1996	November 12, 1997
Poland	September 24, 1996	May 25, 1999
Republic of Korea	September 24, 1996	September 24, 1999
Romania	September 24, 1996	October 5, 1999
Russian Federation	September 24, 1996	June 30, 2000
Slovakia	September 30, 1996	March 3, 1998
South Africa	September 24, 1996	March 30, 1999
Spain	September 24, 1996	July 31, 1998
Sweden	September 24, 1996	December 2, 1998
Switzerland	September 24, 1996	October 1, 1999
Turkey	September 24, 1996	February, 16, 2000
Ukraine	September 27, 1996	February 23, 2001
United Kingdom	September 24, 1996	April 6, 1998
United States	September 24, 1996	
Vietnam	September 24, 1996	

Chapter Eight
Nuclear Terrorism

While the Cold War era was filled with fears of a nuclear holocaust between the Soviet Union and the United States, new nuclear nightmares have emerged at the dawn of the 21st century. Chief among these is the threat of nuclear terrorism. There are many unanswered questions about this potential threat, which is partly the reason for the anxiety it causes. It is unclear and unpredictable if terrorist organizations either (1) possess nuclear weapons, or (2) are developing or attempting to acquire such weapons.

One such terrorist network suspected of possessing nuclear weapons is the Al-Qaeda, led by Osama Bin Laden. This group was responsible for the devastating terrorist attacks of September 11, 2001 on the United States which claimed the lives of over 3,000 people. On that tragic day, the Al-Qaeda terrorists hijacked four passenger airplanes and used them as guided missiles. Two of the planes were crashed into the World Trade Center in New York and one into the Pentagon located just outside Washington, D.C. Only the heroic acts of passengers on Flight 93 prevented the terrorists from guiding another plane into an intended target. The passengers of Flight 93 attacked their hijackers and in the ensuing struggle, the plane went down in a field in Pennsylvania claiming the lives of all on board, but saving perhaps countless others.

The U.S. and its allies immediately embarked on an all-out war on terrorism following the September 11th attacks. As U.S. troops destroyed Al-Qaeda camps in Afghanistan, part of their mission was to uncover clues as to possible terrorist plots against the civilized world. The Central Intelligence Agency (CIA) was also on the hunt for documents that might reveal if Al-Qaeda possessed nuclear weapons.

"More recently, we have uncovered rudimentary diagrams of nuclear weapons inside a suspected al Qa'ida safehouse in Kabul (Afghanistan). These

diagrams, while crude, describe essential components—uranium and high explosives— common to nuclear weapons.[30]

"In 1988, Osama Bin Ladin stated that he considered acquiring weapons of mass destruction a 'religious duty', and recent press reports claim that Bin Ladin has nuclear weapons to use as a deterrent against the United States. A government witness-- Jamal Ahmad Fadl--in the trial of four men recently convicted of supporting the al Qa'ida bombings of the American embassies in Tanzania and Kenya testified last February that al Qa'ida had been trying to acquire fissile material since the early 1990s."[31]

While the CIA's report is unsettling to say the least, it does not provide proof that Al-Qaeda or any other terrorist group possesses nuclear capability. But it does not prove that they do not.

"Although the potential devastation from nuclear terrorism is high, we have no credible reporting on terrorists successfully acquiring nuclear weapons or sufficient material to make them. Gaps in our reporting, however, make this an issue of ongoing concern."[32]

How likely is it that terrorists could actually acquire the necessary material for a nuclear weapon... and then actually build one? Here is one opinion from the director of the International Atomic Energy Agency...

"While we cannot exclude the possibility that terrorists could get hold of some nuclear material,"

---

[30] CIA Report titled "Unclassified Report to Congress On the Acquisition of Technology Relating to Weapons of Mass Destruction and Advanced Conventional Munitions."

[31] Ibid

[32] Ibid

says Mr. El Baradei (IAEA Director General), "it is highly unlikely they could use it to manufacture and successfully detonate a nuclear bomb. Still, no scenario is impossible."[33]

The IAEA in a press release comments further on this issue....

"Beyond the difficulty for terrorists to obtain weapon usable material - scientists estimate that 25 kg of highly enriched uranium or 8 kg of plutonium would be needed to make a bomb - actually producing a nuclear weapon is far from a trivial exercise. Scientific expertise and access to sophisticated equipment would be required."[34]

Another risk posed to the civilized world may be a terrorist attack on a nuclear power plant. Following the September 11th attacks, security was heightened at nuclear facilities throughout the world.

Or another threat is the dispersing of radiation, also known as a "dirty bomb." According to the IAEA, such a bomb could be created by "shrouding conventional explosives around a source containing radioactive material."

Where could terrorists acquire radioactive material?

"The number of radioactive sources around the world is vast.... Many more are used in industry; for example, to check for welding errors or cracks in buildings, pipelines and structures. They are also used for the preservation of food. There is a large number of unwanted radioactive sources, many of them abandoned,..." [35]

---

[33] IAEA Press Release, "Calculating the New Global Nuclear Terrorism Threat" November 1, 2001 (www.iaea.org)
[34] Ibid
[35] Ibid

"Certainly, the effects of a dirty bomb would not be devastating in terms of human life," says Abel Gonzalez, the IAEA's Director of Radiation and Waste Safety, "but contamination in even small quantities could have major psychological and economic effects."[36]

The threats are numerous and they may be prevalent for the duration of the 21st century. Nuclear weapons may not be the most likely method of terrorist attack, as evidenced by the September 11th hijackings. However, nuclear terrorism is potentially the most horrific scenario and therefore should be guarded against vigilantly by the civilized world.

"A lone madman or nest of fanatics with…a crude nuclear bomb can threaten or kill tens of thousands of people in a single act of malevolence. These are not far-off or far-fetched scenarios. They are real-- here and now. …As the new millennium approaches, the United States faces a heightened prospect that regional aggressors, third-rate armies, terrorist cells, and even religious cults will wield disproportionate power by using -- or even threatening to use -- nuclear, biological or chemical weapons against our troops in the field and our people at home…." [37]

---

[36] Ibid
[37] Office of the Secretary of Defense, "Proliferation: Threat and Response," November 1997, Message of the Secretary of Defense, William Cohen, page iii

Chapter Nine
Conclusion

In 1996 the International Court of Justice ruled that nuclear weapons are illegal in accordance with international law. What is the significance of such a ruling? It will not bring about the end of nuclear weapons in the world, but it clearly reiterates the feeling of the world community. Nuclear weapons are inhumane and should be eliminated. This is the ultimate goal of the Non-Proliferation Treaty. But the world has seen its share of laws unenforced and treaties broken. In 1928 the Kellogg-Briand Pact essentially outlawed war between nations. Over sixty nations signed on to this treaty, but we all know the rest of the story. The world was at war within the next decade.

The end to nuclear weapons cannot come about until there is peace among all nations. And as long as nuclear weapons exist, it is less likely that such peace can be achieved.

The United States and Russia must lead the way in bringing about an end to nuclear weapons. They are the original nuclear powers, possess the largest stockpiles, and can exert the most influence in convincing uncommitted nations to end proliferation of these weapons.

At the end of World War II and the dropping of the first atomic bombs on Hiroshima and Nagasaki, the United States assessed the impact of the first nuclear weapons. In a report titled "The Effects of the Atomic Bombings of Hiroshima and Nagasaki," a telling final conclusion outlines the moral obligations of the United States in the future.

> *"No more forceful arguments for peace and for the international machinery of peace than the sight of the devastation of Hiroshima and Nagasaki have ever been devised. As the developer and exploiter of this ominous weapon, our nation has a responsibility, which no American should shirk, to lead in establishing and implementing the international*

guarantees and controls which will prevent its future use. [38]

    The costs of maintaining a nuclear weapons arsenal loom large for any nation. The Department of Energy of the United States reports that 4.6 billion dollars was requested in 2001 for maintaining the safety and reliability of the U.S. nuclear weapons. This program, referred to as stockpile stewardship, is done without explosive nuclear testing. The figure of 4.6 billion is an average of roughly 17 dollars per person in the United States. The costs of conducting actual nuclear test explosions or developing new weapons of mass destruction would only add to this figure. The aforementioned costs do not include expenses for the cleanup of nuclear radioactive waste from prior weapons production. Radioactive waste can be an environmental and health risk for thousands of years. Clearly, as long as a nation possesses nuclear weapons, stockpile stewardship is a necessity. However, that brings the question of how long does a nation wish to own a nuclear weapons arsenal and if so, how large? Nuclear weapons drain resources from society as well as from conventional military forces, which are responsible for a nation's security. Clearly, a nation must analyze its priorities in terms of allocating resources for its national security and for its society.

    "Rome wasn't built in a day," and the same can be said for nuclear disarmament. It will not come about instantaneously. Nations possessing nuclear weapons regard them as deterrents to potential enemies and therefore vital to their national security. With this deterrence factor, you can perhaps keep a peace of sorts, but not a true one. The Joint Chiefs of Staff of the United States recognized this when evaluating the atomic bomb in 1947.

---

[38] United States Strategic Bombing Survey, "The Effects of the Atomic Bombings of Hiroshima and Nagasaki," June 19, 1946, p. 45 (Harry S. Truman Library) See Appendix p. 123.

"A peace enforced through fear is a poor substitute for a peace maintained through international cooperation based upon agreement and understanding."[39]

In conclusion, the words of President John F. Kennedy best describe the path toward nuclear disarmament.

"Let us, if we can, get back from the shadows of war and seek out the way of peace. And if that journey is one thousand miles, or even more, let history record that we, in this land, at this time, took the first step."

---

[39] Joint Chiefs of Staff Evaluation Board for Operation Crossroads, "The Evaluation of the Atomic Bomb as a Military Weapon," p. 13, June 30, 1947.

APPENDIX

The Effects of the Atomic Bombings of
Hiroshima and Nagasaki

Memorandum by the Chief of Staff, U.S. Air
Force, to the Secretary of Defense on Long
Range Detection of Atomic Explosions

Memorandum of Conference With The President
August 14, 1958

Documents on Nuclear Test Ban Negotiations

Facts About Fallout

Worldwide Reaction to Communist China's
Third Nuclear Explosion

Nuclear Arms Reductions: Treaty between the
United States and Russia signed on May 24,
2002 in Moscow

THE UNITED STATES
STRATEGIC BOMBING SURVEY

THE EFFECTS OF

THE ATOMIC BOMBINGS

OF

HIROSHIMA AND NAGASAKI

CHAIRMAN'S OFFICE

19   June   1946

FOREWORD

The United States Strategic Bombing Survey was established
by the Secretary of War on 3 November 1944, pursuant to a Directive
from the late President Roosevelt. Its mission was to conduct an
impartial and expert study of the effects of our aerial attack on
Germany, to be used in connection with air attacks on Japan and to
establish a basis for evaluating the importance and potentialities
of air power as an instrument of military strategy, for planning the
future development of the United States armed forces, and for deter-
mining future economic policies with respect to the national defense.
A summary report and some 200 supporting reports containing the findings of the Survey in Germany have been published.

On 15 August 1945, President Truman requested that the
Survey conduct a similar study of the effects of all types of air
attack in the war against Japan, submitting reports in duplicate to
the Secretary of War and to the Secretary of the Navy. The officers
of the Survey during its Japanese phase were:

> Franklin D'Olier, Chairman
> Paul H. Nitze, Henry C. Alexander, Vice-Chairmen
> Walter Wilds, Secretary
> Harry L. Bowman
> J. K. Galbraith
> Rensis Likert
> Frank A. McNamee
> Fred Searls, Jr.
> Monroe Spaght
> Dr. Louis R. Thompson
> Theodore P. Wright, Directors.

The Survey's complement provided for 300 civilians,
350 officers, and 500 enlisted men. The military segment of the
organization was drawn from the Army to the extent of 60 percent,
and from the Navy to the extent of 40 percent. Both the Army and
Navy gave the Survey all possible assistance in furnishing men,
supplies, transport, and information. The Survey operated from
headquarters in Tokyo early in September, 1945, with sub-headquarters
in Nagoya, Osaka, Hiroshima, and Nagasaki, and with mobile teams
operating in other parts of Japan, the islands of the Pacific and the
Asiatic mainland.

It was possible to reconstruct much of wartime Japanese
military planning and execution engagement by engagement and **campaign**

by campaign, and to secure reasonably accurate statistics on Japan's economy and war-production plant by plant, and industry by industry. In addition, studies were conducted on Japan's overall strategic plans and the background of her entry into the war, the internal discussions and negotiations leading to her acceptance of unconditional surrender, the course of health and morale among the civilian population, the effectiveness of the Japanese civilian defense organization and the effects of the atomic bombs. Separate reports will be issued covering each phase of the study.

The Survey interrogated more than 700 Japanese military, government and industrial officials. It also recovered and translated many documents which have not only been useful to the Survey, but will also furnish data valuable for other studies. Arrangements are being made to turn over the Survey's files to a permanent government agency where they will be available for further examination and distribution.

T A B L E O F C O N T E N T S

I.   INTRODUCTION

The available facts about the power of the atomic bomb as a military weapon lie in the story of what it did at Hiroshima and Nagasaki. Many of these facts have been published, in official and unofficial form, but mingled with distortions or errors. The U. S. Strategic Bombing Survey, therefore, in partial fulfillment of the mission for which it was established, has put together in these pages a fairly full account of just what the atomic bombs did at Hiroshima and Nagasaki. Together with an explanation of how the bomb achieved these effects, this report states the extent and nature of the damage, the casualties, and the political repercussions from the two attacks. The basis is the observation, measurement, and analysis of the Survey's investigators. The conjecture that is necessary for understanding of complex phenomena and for applying the findings to the problems of defense of the U.S. is clearly labelled.

When the atomic bombs fell, the U.S. Strategic Bombing Survey was completing a study of the effects of strategic bombing on Germany's ability and will to resist. A similar study of the effects of strategic bombing on Japan was being planned. The news of the dropping of the atomic bomb gave a new urgency to this project, for a study of the air war against Japan clearly involved new weapons and new possibilities of concentration of attack that might qualify or even change the conclusions and recommendations of the Survey as to the effectiveness of air power. The directors of the Survey, therefore, decided to examine exhaustively the effects of the atomic bombs, in order that the full impact on Japan and the implications of their results could be confidently analyzed. Teams of experts were selected to study the scenes of the bombings from the special points of emphasis of physical damage, civilian defense, morale, casualties, community life, utilities and transportation, various industries, and the general economic and political repercussions. In all, more than 110 men - engineers, architects, fire experts, economists, doctors, photographers, draftsmen - participated in the field study at each city, over a period of ten weeks from October to December, 1945. Their detailed studies, now being published, are listed in an appendix to this summary report.

In addition, close liaison was maintained with other investigating units. Cooperation was received from, and extended to, the following groups:

The Joint Commission for the Investigation of the Atomic Bomb in Japan

79

The British Mission to Japan

The Naval Technical Mission to Japan

Special acknowledgement is due to the medical groups of the Joint Commission, whose data and findings have been generously made available to the Survey. On medical aspects of the bombings, the Joint Commission was the chief fact-finding group; it will present its definitive report in the near future. In other fields, however -- particularly the study of physical damage and the impact on community life -- the Survey collected its own data and is the primary source.

II. The Effects of the Atomic Bombings.

A. The Attacks and Damage.

1. The Attacks.

A single atomic bomb, the first weapon of its type ever used against a target, exploded over the city of Hiroshima at 0815 on the morning of 6 August 1945. Most of the industrial workers had already reported to work, but many workers were enroute and nearly all the school children and some industrial employees were at work in the open on the program of building removal to provide firebreaks and disperse valuables to the country. The attack came 45 minutes after the "all clear" had been sounded from a previous alert. Because of the lack of warning and the populace's indifference to small groups of planes, the explosion came as an almost complete surprise, and the people had not taken shelter. Many were caught in the open, and most of the rest in flimsily constructed homes or commercial establishments.

The bomb exploded slightly northwest of the center of the city. Because of this accuracy and the flat terrain and circular shape of the city, Hiroshima was uniformly and extensively devastated. Practically the entire densely or moderately built-up portion of the city was leveled by blast and swept by fire. A "fire-storm", a phenomenon which has occurred infrequently in other conflagrations, developed in Hiroshima: fires springing up almost simultaneously over the wide flat area around the center of the city drew in air from all directions. The inrush of air easily overcame the natural ground wind, which had a velocity of only about five miles per hour. The "fire-wind" attained a maximum velocity of 30 to 40 miles per hour two to three hours after the explosion. The "fire-wind" and the symmetry of the built-up center of the city gave a roughly circular shape to the 4.4 square miles which were almost completely burned out.

The surprise, the collapse of many buildings, and the conflagration contributed to an unprecedented casualty rate. Seventy to eighty thousand people were killed, or missing and presumed dead, and an equal number were injured. The magnitude of casualties is set in relief by a comparison with the Tokyo fire raid of 9/10 March 1945, in which, though nearly 16 square miles were destroyed, the number killed was no larger and fewer people were injured.

At Nagasaki, three days later, the city was scarcely more prepared, though vague references to the Hiroshima disaster had appeared in the newspaper of 8 August. From the Nagasaki Prefectural Report on the bombing, something of the shock of the explosion can be inferred:

"The day was clear with not very much wind -- an ordinary midsummer's day. The strain of continuous air attack on the city's population and the severity of the summer had vitiated enthusiastic air raid precautions. Previously, a general alert had been sounded at 0748, with a raid alert at 0750; this was cancelled at 0830, and the alertness of the people was dissipated by a great feeling of relief."

The city remained on the warning alert, but when two B-29's were again sighted coming in the raid signal was not given immediately; the bomb was dropped at 1102 and the raid signal was given a few minutes later, at 1109. Thus only about 400 people were in the city's tunnel shelters, which were adequate for about 30 per cent of the population.

> "When the atomic bomb exploded, an intense flash was observed first, as though a large amount of magnesium had been ignited, and the scene grew hazy with white smoke. At the same time at the center of the explosion, and a short while later in other areas, a tremendous roaring sound was heard and a crushing blast wave and intense heat were felt. The people of Nagasaki, even those who lived on the outer edge of the blast, all felt as though they had sustained a direct hit, and the whole city suffered damage such as would have resulted from direct hits everywhere by ordinary bombs."

> "The Zero area where the damage was most severe was almost completely wiped out and for a short while after the explosion no reports came out of that area. People who were in comparatively damaged areas reported their condition under the impression that they had received a direct hit. If such a great amount of damage could be wreaked by a near miss, then the power of the atomic bomb is unbelievably great."

In Nagasaki, no fire storm arose, and the uneven terrain of the city confined the maximum intensity of damage to the valley over which the bomb exploded. The area of nearly complete devastation was thus much smaller: only about 1.8 square miles. Casualties were lower also; between 35,000 and 40,000 were killed, and about the same number injured. People in the tunnel shelters escaped injury, unless exposed in the entrance shaft.

The difference in the totals of destruction to lives and property at the two cities suggests the importance of the special circumstances of layout and construction of the cities, which affect the results of the bombings and must be considered in evaluating the effectiveness of the atomic bombs. An account of the nature and history of each city will give meaning to the details of the damage and disorganization at each.

2. HIROSHIMA.

The city of Hiroshima is located on the broad fan-shaped delta of the Ota River, whose seven mouths divide the city into six

- 4 -

islands which project finger-like into Hiroshima Bay of the Inland Sea. These mouths of the river furnished excellent firebreaks in a city that is otherwise flat and only slightly above sea level. A highly developed bridge system, with 81 important bridges, joined the islands. A single kidney shaped hill in the eastern part of the city, about one-half mile long and rising to an elevation of 221 feet, offered some blast protection to structures on the eastern side opposite the point of fall of the bomb. Otherwise, the city was uniformly exposed to the spreading energy from the bomb.

The city boundary extends to some low hills to the west and northeast and embraces 26.36 square miles, only thirteen of which were built up. Seven square miles were densely or moderately built up, the remainder being occupied by sparsely built-up residential, storage, and transportation areas, vegetable farms, water courses, and wooded hilly sections. In the central area, no systematic separation of commercial, industrial, and residential zones existed, though there were rough functional sections. The main commercial district was located in the center of the city, and with the adjoining Chugoku Regional Army Headquarters occupied the greater portion of the central island. Residential areas and military barracks overlapped and surrounded this central area. The bulk of the industries were located on the perimeter of the city, either on the southern ends of the islands (where the Hiroshima airport was also situated) or to the east of the city. The four square miles of densely built-up area in the heart of the city -- residential, commercial, and military -- contained 75 percent of the total population. If there were, as seems probable, about 245,000 people in the city at the time of the attack, the density in the congested area must have been about 46,000 per square mile. Five completed evacuation programs and a sixth then in progress had reduced the population from its wartime peak of 380,000.

In Hiroshima (and in Nagasaki also) the dwellings were of wood construction; about one-half were one story and the remainder either one and one-half or two stories. The roof coverings were mostly hard-burnt black tile. There were no masonry division walls, and large groups of dwellings clustered together. The type of construction, coupled with antiquated fire-fighting equipment and inadequately trained personnel, afforded even in peacetime a high possibility of conflagration. Many wood framed industrial buildings were of poor construction by American standards. The principal points of weakness were the extremely small tenons, the inadequate tension joints, and the inadequate or poorly designed lateral bracings. Reinforced concrete framed buildings showed a striking lack of uniformity in design and in quality of materials. Some of the construction details (reinforcing rod splices, for example) were often poor, and much of the concrete was definitely weak; thus some reinforced concrete buildings collapsed and suffered structural damage when within 2,000 feet of ground zero, and some internal wall paneling was demolished even up to 3,800 feet. (For convenience, the term "ground zero" will be used to designate the point on the ground directly beneath the point of detonation, or "air zero".)

- 5 -

83

Other buildings, however, were constructed far more strongly than is
required by normal building codes in America, to resist earthquakes.
Furthermore, construction regulations in Japan have specified since
the 1923 earthquake that the roof must safely carry a minimum load of
70 pounds per square foot whereas American requirements do not normally
exceed 40 pounds per square foot for similar types. Though the regula-
tion was not always followed, this extra strong construction was encountered in some of the buildings near ground zero at Hiroshima, and
undoubtedly accounts for their ability to withstand atomic bomb pressures without structural failures. Nearly 7 percent of the residential
units had been torn down to make firebreaks.

Hiroshima before the war was the seventh largest city in
Japan, with a population of over 340,000, and was the principal administrative and commercial center of the southwestern part of the country.
As the headquarters of the Second Army and of the Chugoku Regional Army,
it was one of the most important military command stations in Japan,
the site of one of the largest military supply depots, and the fore-
most military shipping point for both troops and supplies. Its shipping
activities had virtually ceased by the time of the attack, however,
because of sinkings and the mining of the Inland Sea. It had been
relatively unimportant industrially before the war, ranking only
twelfth, but during the war new plants were built that increased its
significance. These factories were not concentrated, but spread over
the outskirts of the city; this location, we shall see, accounts for
the slight industrial damage.

The impact of the atomic bomb shattered the normal fabric
of community life and disrupted the organizations for handling the
disaster. In the 30 percent of the population killed and the additional 30 percent seriously injured were included corresponding proportions
of the civic authorities and rescue groups. A mass flight from the city
took place, as persons sought safety from the conflagration and a place
for shelter and food. Within 24 hours, however, people were streaming
back by the thousands in search of relatives and friends and to determine the extent of their property loss. Road blocks had to be set up
along all routes leading into the city, to keep curious and unauthorized
people out. The bulk of the dehoused population found refuge in the
surrounding countryside; within the city the food supply was short and
shelter virtually non-existent.

On August 7, the commander of the Second Army assumed
general command of the counter-measures, and all military units and
facilities in the area were mobilized for relief purposes. Army
buildings on the periphery of the city provided shelter and emergency
hospital space, and dispersed Army supplies supplemented the slight
amounts of food and clothing that had escaped destruction. The need
far exceeded what could be made available. Surviving civilians assisted;
although casualties in both groups had been heavy, 190 policemen and
over 2000 members of the Civilian Defense Corps reported for duty on

7 August.

The status of medical facilities and personnel dramatically illustrates the difficulties facing authorities. Of more than 200 doctors in Hiroshima before the attack, over 90 percent were casualties and only about 30 physicians were able to perform their normal duties a month after the raid. Out of 1,780 nurses, 1,654 were killed or injured. Though some stocks of supplies had been dispersed, many were destroyed. Only three out of 45 civilian hospitals could be used, and two large Army hospitals were rendered unusable. Those within 3,000 feet of ground zero were totally destroyed, and the mortality rate of the occupants was practically 100 percent. Two large hospitals of reinforced concrete construction were located 4,900 feet from ground zero. The basic structures remained erect but there was such severe interior damage that neither was able to resume operation as a hospital for sometime and the casualty rate was approximately 90 percent, due primarily to falling plaster, flying glass, and fire. Hospitals and clinics beyond 7,000 feet, though often remaining standing, were badly damaged and contained many casualties from flying glass or other missiles.

With such elimination of facilities and personnel, the lack of care and rescue activities at the time of the disaster is understandable; still, the eyewitness account of Father Siemes* shows how this lack of first aid contributed to the seriousness of casualties. At the improvised first aid stations, he reports:

"...Iodine is applied to the wounds but they are left uncleansed. Neither ointment nor other therapeutic agents are available. Those that have been brought in are laid on the floor and no one can give them any further care. What could one do when all means are lacking? Among the passersby, there are many who are uninjured. In a purposeless, insensate manner, distraught by the magnitude of the disaster, most of them rush by and none conceives the thought of organizing help on his own initiative. They are concerned only with the welfare of their own families--in the official aid stations and hospitals, a good third or half of those that had been brought in died. They lay about there almost without care, and a very high percentage succumbed. Everything was lacking, doctors, assistants, dressings, drugs, etc..."

Effective medical help had to be sent in from the outside, and arrived only after a considerable delay.

Fire fighting and rescue units were equally stripped of men and equipment. Father Siemes reports that 30 hours elapsed before any organized rescue parties were observed. In Hiroshima, only 16 pieces of fire-fighting equipment were available for fighting the

* German-born Jesuit professor at Jochi University, Tokyo; in the Hiroshima area when the bomb fell.

- 7 -

conflagration, three of them borrowed. However, it is unlikely that
any public fire department in the world, even without damage to equipment or casualties to personnel, could have prevented development of
a conflagration in Hiroshima, or combatted it with success at more
than a few locations along its perimeter. The total fire damage would
not have been much different.

All utilities and transportation services were disrupted
over varying lengths of time. In most cases, however, the demand fell
off even more precipitously than the available supply, and where the
service was needed it could be restored at a minimal level. Thus,
through railroad service was possible on 8 August, only two days after
the attack, when fire trucks still had to be used to pump water into
the locomotives because of insufficient water pressure. Electric
power from the general network was available in most of the surviving
parts of the city on 7 August, and only one plant, the Engineering
Division of Mitsubishi Heavy Industries, was hampered in its recovery
by the inability to obtain sufficient power for several weeks.

The water reservoir, which was of reinforced concrete and
earthcovered, was undamaged; it was nearly two miles from the blast
center. However, 70,000 breaks of pipe connections in buildings and
dwellings were caused by blast and fire effects. No subsurface pipes
were crushed and no leaks resulted from blast as a direct cause, though
several leaks in underground mains resulted from falling debris.
Pressure in the city center dropped to zero because of the connection
breaks and the damage to a 16-inch and a 14-inch water main where they
crossed damaged bridges. Six sewer pumping stations were rendered
inoperable by fire and blast within a radius of one mile. The remaining eight stations were only slightly damaged, but no effort was made
to repair or operate them. Water tables rose at flood periods and
lands behind revetments were inundated.

Trolley cars, trucks, and railroad rolling stock suffered
extensive damage. Transportation buildings (offices, stations, living
quarters, and a few warehouses) were damaged by fire in the passenger
station area, but damage was slight to the roundhouses, transit sheds,
warehouses, and repair units in the classification and repair area.
About 200 railroad employees were killed, but by 20 August, 14 days after
the attack, 80 percent of the employees were at work.

The electric power transmission and distribution system
was wrecked; only power equipment of rugged construction, such as trans-
formers, resisted the blast and heat within the devastated areas. In-
struments were damaged beyond repair, and switches, switchyard insula-
tors, cables, and copper bus work were rendered unusable. The telephone system was approximately 80 percent damaged, and no service was
restored until 15 August 1945.

Industry in the center of the city was effectively wiped

- 8 -

86

out. Though small workshops numbered several thousand, they represented only one-fourth of the total industrial production of Hiroshima, since many of them had only one or two workers. The bulk of the city's output came from large plants located on the outskirts of the city; one-half of the industrial production came from only five firms. Of these larger companies, only one suffered more than superficial damage. Of their working force, 94 percent were uninjured. Since electric power was available, and materials and working force were not destroyed, plants ordinarly responsible for nearly three-fourths of Hiroshima's industrial production could have resumed normal operation within 30 days of the attack had the war continued.

Immediately after the attack, the presence of these nearly intact industries spurred counter-measures in an effort to retain for the nation's war effort the potential output of the city. The prefectural governor issued a proclamation on 7 August, calling for "a rehabilitation of the stricken city and an aroused fighting spirit to exterminate the devilish Americans". To prevent the spread of rumors and brace morale, 210,000 out-of-town newspapers were brought in daily to replace the destroyed local paper. With the surrender, however, reconstruction took on a slower tempo. On 16 August, regular rationing was resumed. Care of the injured and disposal of corpses remained urgent, but other steps were few.

By 1 November, the population of Hiroshima was back to 137,000. The city required complete rebuilding. The entire heart, the main administrative and commercial as well as residential section, was gone. In this area only about fifty buildings, all of reinforced concrete, remained standing. All of these suffered blast damage and all save about a dozen were almost completely gutted by fire; only five could be used without major repairs. These burnt-out structural frames rose impressively from the ashes of the burned over section where occasional piles of rubble or twisted steel skeletons marked the location of brick or steel frame structures. At greater distances light steel frame and brick structures remained undamaged. Blast damage to wood frame buildings and to residences extended well beyond the burned over area, gradually becoming more erratic and spotty as distances were reached where only the weakest buildings were damaged, until in the outer portions of the city only minor disturbances of the tile roofs or breakage of glass were visible. The official Japanese figures summed up the building destruction at 62,000 out of a total of 90,000 buildings in the urban area, or 69%. An additional 6,000 or 6.6% were severely damaged, and most of the others showed glass breakage or disturbance of roof tile. These figures show the magnitude of the problem facing the survivors.

Despite the absence of sanitation measures, no epidemics are reported to have broken out. In view of the lack of medical facilities, supplies and personnel, and the disruption of the sanitary system, the escape from epidemics may seem surprising. The experience of

- 9 -

other bombed cities in Germany and Japan shows that this is not an
isolated case. A possible explanation may lie in the disinfecting
action of the extensive fires. In later weeks, disease rates rose,
but not sharply.

3. Nagasaki.

Nagasaki is located on the best natural harbor of
western Kyushu, a spacious inlet in the mountainous coast. The city
is a highly congested urban pattern extending for several miles along the narrow shores and up the valleys opening out from the harbor.
Two rivers, divided by a mountain spur, form the two main valleys in
whose basins the city lies: the Urakami River, in whose basin the
atomic bomb fell, running into the harbor from a NNW direction, and
the Nakashima River, running from the NE. This mountain spur and the
irregular lay-out of the city effectively reduced the area of destruction.

The main residential and commercial districts are
intermingled in these two river basins. The large industrial plants
stretch up the west shore of the bay and up the Urakami Valley.
Though the metropolitan area of the city is officially about 35 square
miles and stretches far into the countryside, the heavily built-up
area is confined by the terrain to less than four square miles. The
greatest population density thus approximated 65,000 per square mile
even after the evacuations.

Despite its excellent harbor, Nagasaki's commercial
importance, though great in previous centuries, had declined in recent
years because of the city's isolated peninsular position and the difficulties of transportation through the mountains by inadequate roads
and railroad facilities. As a naval base it had been supplanted by
Sasebo. Industry gradually increased in importance, primarily under
Mitsubishi influence. The four largest companies in the city were the
Mitsubishi Shipyards, Electrical Equipment Works, Arms Plant, and Steel
Works, employing nearly 90 percent of the city's labor force. Admin-
istratively, Nagasaki was by 1941 of merely local importance despite
being the seat of the prefectural government.

Before the atomic bombing on 9 August, Nagasaki had
experienced five small-scale air attacks in the previous twelve months,
by an aggregate of 136 planes which dropped a total of 270 tons of high
explosive, 53 tons of incendiary, and 20 tons of fragmentation bombs.

Of these, a raid of 1 August 1945 was most effective,
with several bombs falling in the Mitsubishi Shipyards and Steel Works.
The scale of effect can be roughly measured, however, by comparing the
toll of building damage with that from the atomic bomb; in all these
raids 276 residential buildings and 21 industrial buildings were destroyed or badly damaged. When the atomic bomb fell, Nagasaki was comparatively intact.

Because the most intense destruction was confined to the Urakami Valley, the impact of the bomb on the city as a whole was less shattering than at Hiroshima. In addition, no fire storm occurred; indeed, a shift in wind direction helped control the fires. Medical personnel and facilities were hard-hit, however. Over 80 percent of the city's hospital beds and the Medical College were located within 3,000 feet of the center of the explosion, and were completely destroyed. Reinforced concrete buildings within this range, though standing, were completely gutted by fire; buildings of wooden construction were destroyed by fire and blast. The mortality rate in this group of buildings was between 75 and 80 percent. Exact casualty figures for medical personnel are unknown, but the city seems to have fared better than Hiroshima: 120 doctors were at work on 1 November, about one-half of the pre-raid roster. Casualties were undoubtedly high: 600 out of 850 medical students at the Nagasaki Medical Collete were killed and most of the others injured; and of the 20 faculty members 12 were killed and four others injured.

Utilities and services were again disrupted. Both gas plants were destroyed, and the replacement time was estimated at several months. Though the basic water supply was not affected, thousands of residential feeder-line breaks were supplemented by eight breaks on a fourteen-inch main li and four breaks where another main line crossed a bridge. Electric power distribution and transmission systems were effectively destroyed in the area of heaviest destruction, but power could be supplied to the other parts of the city almost immediately.

Shipping was virtually unaffected. Trolley service was halted both by the interruption in power supply and by damage to street cars. Nagasaki is at the end of a railroad spur line. The major damage was sustained by track and railroad bridges. The rails buckled intermittently for a distance of 5,000 to 7,500 feet from ground zero, at points where burning debris set fire to wooden cross ties. Three bridges were displaced; rails were distorted and the tracks had to be completely rebuilt. The railroad stations were completely destroyed by blast and fire and the electric signal system was severely damaged. Rolling stock was slightly damaged, primarily by fire. Although the damage to equipment was not extensive, it was severe enough to curtail traffic for 48 hours, during which time sufficient emergency repair work was performed to permit resumption of limited traffic.

Control of relief measures was in the hands of the Prefecture. The sequence of clearance and repair activities illustrates the activities that were carried on.

The city's repair facilities were completely disorganized by the atomic bomb, so that with the single exception of shutting off water to the affected areas no repairs were made to roads, bridges, water mains, or transportation installations by city forces. The prefecture took full responsibility for such restoration as was accomplished,

- 11 -

delegating to the scattered city help the task of assisting in relief of victims. There were only three survivors of 115 employees of the street car company, and late as the middle of November 1945 no cars were running. A week after the explosion, the water works officials made an effort to supply water to persons attempting to live in the bombed out areas, but the leakage was so great that the effort was abandoned. It fell to the prefecture, therefore, to institute recovery measures even in those streets normally the responsibility of the city. Of the entire public works construction group covering the Nagasaki City area, only three members appeared for work and a week was required to locate and notify other survivors. On the morning of 10 August, police rescue units and workers from the Kawami-nami shipbuilding works began the imperative task of clearing the Omura-Nagasaki pike, which was impassable for 8,000 feet. A path 6½ feet wide was cleared despite the intense heat from smouldering fires, and by August 15 had been widened to permit two-way traffic. No trucks, only rakes and shovels, were available for clearing the streets, which were filled with tile, bricks, stone, corrugated iron, machinery, plaster, and stucco. Street areas affected by blast and not by fire were littered with wood. Throughout the devastated area, all wounded had to be carried by stretcher, since no motor vehicles were able to proceed through the cluttered streets for several days. The plan for debris removal required clearance of a few streets leading to the main highway; but there were frequent delays caused by the heat of smouldering fires and by calls for relief work. The debris was simply raked and shoveled off the streets. By 20 August the job was considered complete. The streets were not materially damaged by the bomb nor were the surface or the abutments of the concrete bridges, but many of the wooden bridges were totally or partially destroyed by fire.

Under the circumstances -- fire, flight of entire families, destruction of official records, mass cremation--identification of dead and the accurate count of casualties was impossible. As at Hiroshima, the season of the year made rapid disposal of bodies imperative, and mass cremation and mass burial were resorted to in the days immediately after the attack. Despite the absence of sanitary measures, no epidemics broke out here. The dysentery rate rose from 25/100,000 to 125/100,000. A census taken on 1 November 1945 found a population of 142,700 in the city.

At Nagasaki, the scale of destruction was greater than at Hiroshima, though the actual area destroyed was smaller because of the terrain and the point of fall of the bomb. The Nagasaki Prefectural Report describes vividly the impress of the bomb on the city and its inhabitants:

"Within a radius of one kilometer from ground zero, men and animals died almost instantaneously from the tremendous blast pressure and heat; houses and other structures were smashed, crushed and scattered; and fires broke out. The strong complex steel members of the structures of the Mitsubishi Steel Works were bent and twisted like jelly and the roofs of the reinforced concrete National Schools were crumpled and collapsed, indicating a force beyond imagination. Trees of all sizes lost their branches or were uprooted or broken off at the trunk.

"Outside a radius of one kilometer and within a radius of two kilometers from ground zero, some men and animals died instantly from the great blast and heat, but the great majority were seriously or superficially injured. Houses and other structures were completely destroyed while fires broke out everywhere. Trees were uprooted and withered by the heat.

"Outside a radius of two kilometers and within a radius of four kilometers from ground zero men and animals suffered various degrees of injury from window glass and other fragments scattered about by the blast and many were burned by the intense heat. Dwelling and other structures were half damaged by blast.

"Outside a radius of four kilometers and within a radius of eight kilometers from ground zero living creatures were injured by materials blown about by the blast; the majority were only superficially wounded. Houses were half or only partially damaged."

While the conflagration with its uniformly burnt out area caught the attention at Hiroshima, the blast effects, with their resemblance to the aftermath of a hurricane, were most striking at Nagasaki. Concrete buildings had their sides facing the blast stove in like boxes. Long lines of steel framed factory sheds, over a mile from ground zero, leaned their skeletons away from the explosion. Blast resistant objects like telephone poles leaned away from the center of the explosion; on the surrounding hills trees were blown down within considerable areas. Although there was no general conflagration, fires contributed to the total damage in nearly all concrete structures. Evidence of primary fire is more frequent than at Hiroshima.

Because parts of the city were protected by hills, more than one-half of the residential units escaped serious damage. Of the 52,000 residential units in the city on 1 August, 14,146 or 27.2 percent were completely destroyed (by Japanese count) (11,494 of these were burned); 5,441 or 10.5 percent were half-burned or destroyed; many of the remaining units suffered superficial or minor damage. In 558 non-residential buildings in the built-up area of Nagasaki which the Survey studied, almost 60 percent of the usable floor area was destroyed or structurally damaged. Only 12 percent was undamaged, the rest suffering superficial or minor damage.

The survival of a higher percentage of the buildings, then, distinguishes Nagasaki from Hiroshima; so also, on the other hand, does the damage to factories. In Nagasaki, only the Mitsubishi Dockyards among the major industries was remote enough from the explosion to escape serious damage. The other three Mitsubishi firms, which were responsible together with the dockyards for over 90 percent of the industrial output of the city, were seriously damaged. The Arms Plant and the Steel Works were in the main area of damage. Plant officials estimated that 58 percent of the value of the former and 78 percent of the value of the latter were destroyed: Survey investigators considered the two plants to be 50 percent destroyed. The Mitsubishi Electric Works were on the edge of the main area of destruction, but suffered 10 percent structural damage.

One or two paragraphs from the report of the commanding officer of Sasebo Naval District will illustrate the sort of damage done to industrial installations. Of two plants of the Mitsubishi Arms Works, he reports: ·

"With the exception of the tunnel workshops and the half-underground workshops, the Ohashi and Mori Machi Plants were completely destroyed by collapse. Reinforced concrete structures in these plants were severely damaged internally - ceilings collapsed, fittings of all sorts were destroyed, and equipment was damaged. Casting and forging shops in the Ohashi Plant were destroyed by fire, which broke out in those structures. The Mori Machi Plant was nearly completely destroyed by fire. Taking both plants together, 60% of the machinery installations was damaged. In the Ohashi Plant, from 80 to 90% of the machinery can be used again; in the Mori Machi Plant only 40 to 50% of the machinery can be used in the future."

Or of the Mitsubishi Steel Works:

"Plant structures here (some north-light steel framed structures) suffered extensive damage to roofs and walls as steel plates were blown off. The frames themselves were bent, twisted, or toppled over, and several buildings caught fire. Hardly any of the machinery in the plant can be used again in its present condition. However, nearly 70% of the machinery· can be repaired."

In general, (as has proved true with high explosive or incendiary bombs also), the damage to machinery and other contents of a factory was less than damage to the buildings. In addition, the air burst of the atomic bomb meant that it acted <u>indirectly</u> on machine tools and other building contents. Though a few tools were blown over by blast, almost all the serious damage was caused by debris from damaged buildings, overturning through mass movement of buildings, or burning of buildings.

Thus the extent and sort of damage to machinery depended on the construction of the buildings housing them. In wood frome buildings, 95 percent of the machines were seriously damaged, but in reinforced

- 14 -

concrete or steel framed buildings only one-third or one-fourth of the machines were affected seriously. As would be expected, fire caused much damage to machines in timber framed shops (practically all of which were destroyed up to 7,000 feet from ground zero) and some damage in other types of structure. Debris was a major cause of damage only in certain reinforced concrete buildings, where walls and roofs collapsed.

Shortage of raw materials had reduced operations at these four Mitsubishi plants to a fraction of their capacity. Had the raw material situation been normal and had the war continued, it is estimated that restoration of production would have been possible though slow. The dockyard, which was affected mainly by the 1 August attack rather than by the atomic bomb, would have been able to produce at 80 percent of full capacity within three or four months. The steel works would have required a year to get into substantial production, the electric works could have resumed production at a reduced rate within two months and been back at capacity within six months, and the arms plants would have required 15 months to reach two-thirds of their former capacity.

B. GENERAL EFFECTS

1. Casualties

The most striking result of the atomic bombs was the great number of casualties. The exact number of dead and injured will never be known because of the confusion after the explosions. Persons unaccounted for might have been burned beyond recognition in the falling buildings, disposed of in one of the mass cremations of the first week of recovery, or driven out of the city to die or recover without any record remaining. No sure count of even the pre-raid populations existed. Because of the decline in activity in the two port cities, the constant threat of incendiary raids, and the formal evacuation programs of the government, an unknown number of the inhabitants had either drifted away from the cities or been removed according to plan. In this uncertain situation, estimates of casualties have generally ranged between 100,000 and 180,000 for Hiroshima, and between 50,000 and 100,000 for Nagasaki. The Survey believes the dead at Hiroshima to have been between 70,000 and 80,000, with an equal number injured; at Nagasaki over 35,000 dead and somewhat more than that injured seem the most plausible estimate.

Most of the immediate casualties did not differ from those caused by incendiary or high explosive raids. The outstanding difference was the presence of radiation effects, which became unmistakable about a week after the bombing. At the time of impact, however, the causes of death and injury were flash burns, secondary effects of blast and falling debris, and burns from blazing buildings. No records are available that give the relative importance of the various types of injury, especially for those who died immediately after the explosion. Indeed, many of these people undoubtedly died several times over, theoretically, since each was subjected to several injuries any one of which would have been fatal. The Hiroshima prefectural health department placed the proportion of deaths from burns (flash or flame) at 60 percent, from falling debris at 30 percent and from other injuries at 10 percent; it is generally agreed that burns caused at least 50 percent of the initial casualties. Of those who died later, an increasing proportion succumbed to radiation effects.

The seriousness of these radiation effects may be measured by the fact that 95 percent of the traced survivors of the immediate explosion who were within 3,000 feet suffered from radiation disease. Colonel Stafford Warren, in his testimony before the Senate Committee on Atomic Energy, estimated that radiation was responsible for 7 to 8 percent of the total deaths in the two cities. Most medical investigators who spent some time in the areas feel that this estimate is far too low; it is generally felt that no less than 15 to 20 percent of the deaths were from radiation. In addition, there were an equal number who were casualties but survived, as well as uncounted thousands who probably were affected by the gamma rays but not enough to produce definite illness.

A plausible estimate of the importance of the various causes of death would range as follows:

- 16 -

Flash burns	20 to 30 per cent
Other injuries	50 to 60 per cent
Radiation Sickness	15 to 20 per cent

If we examine the nature of the casualties under each group of causes we find familiar and unfamiliar effects.

Flash burns.

The flash of the explosion, which was extremely brief, emitted radiant heat travelling at the speed of light. Flash burns thus followed the explosion instantaneously. The fact that relatively few victims suffered burns of the eyeballs should not be interpreted as an indication that the radiant heat followed the flash, or that time was required to build up to maximum heat intensity. The explanation is simply that the structure of the eye is more resistant to heat than is average human skin, and near ground zero the recessed position of the eyeball offered protection from the overhead explosion. Peak temperatures lasted only momentarily.

Survivors in the two cities stated that people who were in the open directly under the explosion of the bomb were so severely burned that the skin was charred dark brown or black and that they died within a few minutes or hours.

Among the survivors, the burned areas of the skin showed evidence of burns almost immediately after the explosion. At first there was marked redness, and other evidence of thermal burns appeared within the next few minutes or hours, depending on the degree of the burn. Uninfected burns healed promptly without any unusual clinical features, according to the Japanese physicians who attended the cases. American medical observers noted only a tendency to formation of excess scar tissue, which could be satisfactorily explained as the result of malnutrition and the large degree of secondary infection that complicated healing of the burns. There were also a few instances of burns healing with contractures and limitation of the mobility of certain joints, such as the elbows or knees. In many instances, these primary burns of minor nature were completely healed before patients developed evidence of radiation effects.

Because of the brief duration of the flash wave and the shielding effects of almost any objects -- leaves and clothing as well as buildings- there were many interesting cases of protection. The radiant heat came in a direct line like light, so that the area burned corresponded to this directed exposure. Persons whose sides were toward the explosion often showed definite burns of both sides of the back while the hollow of the back escaped. People in buildings or houses were apparently burned only if directly exposed through the windows. The most striking instance was that of a man writing before a window. His hands were seriously burned but his exposed face and neck suffered only slight burns due to the angle of entry of the radiant heat through the window.

Flash burns were largely confined to exposed areas of the body, but on occasion would occur through varying thicknesses of clothing. Generally speaking, the thicker the clothing the more likely it was to give complete protection against flash burns. One woman was burned over the shoulder except for a T-shaped area about one-fourth inch in breadth; the T-shaped area corresponded to an increased thickness of the clothing from the seam of the garment. Other people were burned through a single thickness of kimono but were unscathed or only lightly affected underneath the lapel. In other instances, skin was burned beneath tightly fitting clothing but was unburned beneath loosely fitting portions. Finally, white or light colors reflected heat and afforded some protection; people wearing black or dark-colored clothing were more likely to be burned.

Other Injuries

Because of the combination of factors at the area near the center of the explosion, the casualty effects of blast are hard to single out. If it is remembered that even directly under the explosion people were several hundred feet away from the air-burst, it will be easier to understand why true blast effects were relatively rare. Only toward the periphery of the affected zone was the blast effect lateral and likely to throw people violently against buildings, and at the periphery the intensity of the blast had fallen off sharply. Comparatively few instances were reported of arms or legs being torn from the body by flying debris. Another indication of the rarity of over-pressure is the scarcity of ruptured eardrums. Among 106 victims examined by the Japanese in Hiroshima on 11 and 12 August, only three showed ruptured eardrums; a study done in October at the Omura hospital near Nagasaki revealed that only two of 92 cases had ruptured eardrums. Only at Nagasaki were there reports of over-pressure in the stock wave. Some of the dead were said by survivors to have had their abdomens ruptured and intestines protruding; others were reported to have protruding eyes and tongues, and to have looked as if they had drowned. Thorough check by Allied investigators discredited these stories as evidence of direct blast effects; the normal effects of blast are internal hemorrhage and crushing. These external signs point to injuries from debris rather than blast.

Injuries produced by falling and flying debris were much more numerous, and naturally increased in number and seriousness nearer the center of the affected area. The collapse of the buildings was sudden, so that thousands of people were pinned beneath the debris. Many were able to extricate themselves or received aid in escaping, but large numbers succumbed either to their injuries or to fire before they could be extricated. The flimsiness of Japanese residential construction should not be allowed to obscure the dangers of collapse; though the walls and partitions were light, the houses had heavy roof timbers and heavy roof tiles. Flying glass from panels also caused a large number of casualties, even up to 15,000 feet from ground zero.

The number of burns from secondary fires was slight among survivors, but it was probable that a large number of the deaths in both cities came

from the burning of people caught in buildings. Eyewitness accounts agree
that many fatalities occurred in this way, either immediately or as a result of the lack of care for those who did extricate themselves with serious burns. There are no references, however, to people in the streets
succumbing either to heat or to carbon monoxide as they did in Tokyo or
in Hamburg, Germany. A few burns resulted from clothing set afire by the
flash wave, but in most cases people were able to beat out such fires
without serious injury to the skin.

Radiation Disease

The radiation effects upon survivors resulted from the gamma rays
liberated by the fission process rather than from induced radio-activity
or the lingering radio-activity of deposits of primary fission products.
Both at Nagasaki and at Hiroshima, pockets of radio-activity have been
detected where fission products were directly deposited, but the degree
of activity in these areas was insufficient to produce casualties. Similarly, induced radio-activity from the interaction of neutrons with matter
caused no authenticated fatalities. But the effects of gamma rays --
here used in a general sense to include all penetrating high-frequency
radiations and neutrons that caused injury-- are well established, even
though the Allies had no observers in the affected areas for several weeks
after the explosions.

Our understanding of radiation casualties is not complete. In part
the deficiency is in our basic knowledge of how radiation affects animal
tissue. In the words of Dr. Robert Stone of the Manhattan Project, "The
fundamental mechanism of the action of radiation on living tissues has
not been understood. All methods of treatment have therefore been sym-
ptomatic rather than specific. For this reason, studies into the fundamental nature of the action of radiation have been carried on to some extent, the limitation being that it was unlikely that significant results
could be obtained during the period of war."

According to the Japanese, those individuals very near the center of
the explosion but not affected by flash burns or secondary injuries became
ill within two or three days. Bloody diarrhea followed, and the victims
expired, some within two to three days after the onset and the majority
within a week. Autopsies showed remarkable changes in the blood picture--
almost complete absence of white blood cells, and deterioration of bone
marrow. Mucous membranes of the throat, lungs, stomach, and intestines
showed acute inflammation.

The majority of the radiation cases, who were at greater distances,
did not show severe symptoms until one to four weeks after the explosion,
though many felt weak and listless on the following day. After a day or
two of mild nausea and vomiting, the appetite improved and the person felt
quite well until symptoms reappeared at a later date. In the opinion of
some Japanese physicians, those who rested or subjected themselves to less
physical exertion showed a longer delay before the onset of subsequent
symptoms. The first signs of recurrence were loss of appetite, lassitude,

and general discomfort. Inflammation of the gums, mouth, and pharynx appeared next. Within 12 to 48 hours, fever became evident. In many instances it reached only 100° Fahrenheit and remained for only a few days. In other cases, the temperature went as high as 104° or 106° Fahrenheit. The degree of fever apparently had a direct relation to the degree of exposure to radiation. Once developed, the fever was usually well sustained, and in those cases terminating fatally it continued high until the end. If the fever subsided, the patient usually showed a rapid disappearance of other symptoms and soon regained his feeling of good health. The other symptoms commonly seen were shortage of white corpuscles, loss of hair, inflammation and gangrene of the gums, inflammation of the mouth and pharynx, ulceration of the lower gastrointestinal tract, small livid spots (petechiae) resulting from escape of blood into the tissues of the skin or mucous membrane, and larger hemorrhages of gums, nose and skin.

Loss of hair usually began about two weeks after the bomb explosion, though in a few instances it is reported to have begun as early as four to five days afterwards. The areas were involved in the following order, with variations depending on the degree of exposure: scalp, armpits, beard, pubic region, and eyebrows. Complete baldness was rare. Microscopic study of the body areas involved has shown atrophy of the hair follicles. In those patients who survived after two months, however, the hair has commenced to regrow. An interesting but unconfirmed report has it that loss of the hair was less marked in persons with grey hair than in those with dark hair.

A decrease in the number of white blood corpuscles in the circulating blood appears to have been a constant accompaniment of radiation disease, even existing in some milder cases without other radiation effects. The degree of leukopenia was probably the most accurate index of the amount of radiation a person received. The normal white blood count averages 5,000 to 7,000: leukopenia is indicated by a count of 4,000 or less. The white blood count in the more severe cases ranged from 1,500 to 0, with almost entire disappearance of the bone marrow. The moderately severe cases showed evidence of degeneration of bone marrow and total white blood counts of 1,500 to 3,000. The milder cases showed white blood counts of 3,000 to 4,000 with more minor degeneration changes in the bone marrow. The changes in the system for forming red blood corpuscles developed later, but were equally severe.

Radiation clearly affected reproduction, though the extent has not been determined. Sterility has been a common finding throughout Japan, especially under the conditions of the last two years, but there are signs of an increase in the Hiroshima and Nagasaki areas to be attributed to the radiation. Sperm counts done in Hiroshima under American supervision revealed low sperm counts or complete aspermia for as long as three months afterwards in males who were within 5,000 feet of the center of the explosion. Cases dying of radiation disease showed clear effects on spermatogenesis. Study of sections of ovaries from autopsied radiation victims has not yet been completed. The effects of the bomb on pregnant women are marked, however. Of women in various stages of pregnancy who were

within 3,000 feet of ground zero, all known cases have had miscarriages. Even up to 6,500 feet they have had miscarriages or premature infants who died shortly after birth. In the group between
6,500 feet and 10,000 feet, about one-third have given birth to
apparently normal children. Two months after the explosion, the city's
total incidence of miscarriages, abortions, and premature births was
27 per cent as compared with a normal rate of 6 per cent. Since other
factors than radiation contributed to this increased rate, a period
of years will be required to learn the ultimate effects of mass
radiation upon reproduction.

Treatment of victims by the Japanese was limited by the lack of
medical supplies and facilities. Their therapy consisted of small
amounts of vitamins, liver extract, and an occasional blood trans-
fusion. Allied doctors used penicillin and plasma with beneficial
effects. Liver extract seemed to benefit the few patients on whom
it was used: it was given in small frequent doses when available.
A large percentage of the cases died of secondary disease, such as
septic bronchopneumonia or tuberculosis, as a result of lowered
resistance. Deaths from radiation began about a week after exposure
and reached a peak in three to four weeks. They had practically
ceased to occur after seven to eight weeks.

Unfortunately, no exact definition of the killing power of
radiation can yet be given, nor a satisfactory account of the sort and
thickness of concrete or earth that will shield people. From the
definitive report of the Joint Commission will come more nearly
accurate statements on these matters. In the meanwhile the awesome
lethal effects of the atomic bomb and the insidious additional peril
of the gamma rays speak for themselves.

There is reason to believe that if the effects of blast and fire
had been entirely absent from the bombing, the number of deaths among
people within a radius of one-half mile from ground zero would have
been almost as great as the actual figures and the deaths among those
within one mile would have been only slightly less. The principal
difference would have been in the time of the deaths. Instead of
being killed outright as were most of these victims, they would have
survived for a few days or even three or four weeks, only to die
eventually of radiation disease.

These suppositions have vital importance, for actually in Nagasaki
and Hiroshima many people who were protected by structures against blast
and fire were not protected against the effect of gamma rays. The complexity of the problem of shelter protection has been increased by this
necessity of shielding against radiant heat and gamma rays. Fortunately,
earth and concrete will shield against gamma rays, the required thickness
varying with the intensity of the rays.

The slow and inadequate treatment of victims by the Japanese probably contributed to the high casualty rates. Many persons could undoubtedly have been saved had facilities, supplies and personnel been
available immediately after the bombings. Probably the number of deaths
from the true blast effects, flame burns, or serious injuries from coll-
apsing structures would not have been altered appreciably; generally
speaking, these cases either were killed outright or else survived.
Many of the flash burn cases could have been saved with tremendous quantities of plasma and parenteral fluids if treatment could have begun within a few hours after the bombing. Probably the most significant results
could have been achieved with the radiation cases. With large quantities
of whole blood and adequate supportive treatment, possibly 10 to 20 percent of those dying of radiation might have survived. However, it is
doubtful that 10 percent of all the deaths resulting from the atomic
bombs could have been avoided with the best medical care. A more likely
figure is 5 to 8 percent.

100

2. Morale*

As might be expected, the primary reaction to the bomb was fear -- uncontrolled terror, strengthened by the sheer horror of the destruction and suffering witnessed and experienced by the survivors. Between one-half and two-thirds of those interviewed in the Hiroshima and Nagasaki areas confessed having such reactions, not just for the moment but for some time. As two survivors put it:

"Whenever a plane was seen after that, people would rush into their shelters: they went in and out so much that they did not have time to eat. They were so nervous they could not work."

"After the atomic bomb fell, I just couldn't stay home. I would cook, but while cooking I would always be watching out and worrying whether an atomic bomb would fall near me."

The behavior of the living immediately after the bombings, as described earlier, clearly shows the state of shock that hindered rescue efforts. A Nagasaki survivor illustrates succinctly the mood of survivors:

"All I saw was a flash and I felt my body get warm and then I saw everything flying around. My grandmother was hit on the head by a flying piece of roof and she was bleeding . . . I became hysterical seeing my grandmother bleeding and we just ran around without knowing what to do."

"I was working at the office. I was talking to a friend at the window. I saw the whole city in a red flame, then I ducked. The pieces of the glass hit my back and face. My dress was torn off by the glass. Then I got up and ran to the mountain where the good shelter was."

The two typical impulses were those: aimless, even hysterical activity, or flight from the city to shelter and food.

The accentuated effect of these bombs came not only from the surprise and their crushing power, but also from the feeling of security among the inhabitants of the two cities before the attacks. Though Nagasaki had undergone five raids in the previous year, they had not been heavy, and Hiroshima had gone almost untouched until the morning of 6 August 1945. In both cities many people felt that they would be spared, and the various rumors in circulation supporting such feeling covered a wide range of wishful thoughts. There were so many Christians

* A U.S.S.B.S. Morale division team interviewed a scientifically selected sample of almost 250 persons: 128 from Hiroshima and Nagasaki cities, and 120 from the immediately surrounding areas. The same standard questions were put to these people and similar groups in representative Japanese cities.

there, many Japanese-Americans came from Hiroshima, the city was a
famous beauty spot --these and other even more fantastic reasons encouraged hopes. Other people felt vaguely that their city was being
saved for "something big", however.

Such a shattering event could not fail to have its impact on people's
ways of thinking. Study of the patterns of belief about the war, before
and after the bombing, show this change clearly. Prior to the dropping
of the atomic bombs, the people of the two target cities appear to have
had fewer misgivings about the war than people in other cities.
Responses to set questions indicate that among Japanese civilians prior
to 1 July 1945

    59% in the Hiroshima-Nagasaki areas
       but
    74% in the other urban areas
       entertained doubts about a Japanese Victory;
    31% in Hiroshima-Nagasaki
       but
    47% in other urban areas
       felt certain that victory for Japan was impossible;
    12% in Hiroshima-Nagasaki
       but
    34% in other urban areas
       had reached a point where they felt unable to continue the war.
Further,
    28% of the people of Japan as a whole said they had never reached
       a point where they felt they could not go on with the war
       whereas
    39% of the people in the Hiroshima-Nagasaki areas said they had
       never reached such a point.

These figures clearly suggest that the will to resist had indeed been
higher in the "atomic bomb cities" than in Japan as a whole.

There is no doubt that the bomb was the most important influence
among the people of these areas in making them think that defeat was
inevitable. An additional twenty-eight percent stated that after the
atomic bomb was dropped they became convinced that victory for Japan
was impossible. Almost one-fourth admitted that because of the bombing
they felt personally unable to carry on. Forty percent testified to
various degrees of defeatism induced by the atomic bomb. Significantly,
certainty of defeat was much more prevalent at Hiroshima, where the area
of devastation and the casualties were greater, than at Nagasaki.

Typical comments of survivors were:

    "If the enemy has this type of bomb, everyone is going to die, and
    we wish the war would hurry and finish."

"I did not expect that it was that powerful. I thought we have no defense against such a bomb."

"One of my children was killed by it, and I didn't care what happened after that."

Other reactions were found. In view of their experiences, it is not remarkable that some of the survivors (nearly one-fifth) hated the Americans for using the bomb or expressed their anger in such terms as "cruel", "inhuman", and "barbarous".

". . they really despise the Americans for it, the people all say that if there are such things as ghosts, why don't they haunt the Americans?"

"When I saw the injured and killed, I felt bitter against the enemy."

"After the atomic bomb exploded, I felt that now I must go to work in a munitions plant. . . My sons told me that they wouldn't forget the atomic bomb even when they grow up."

The reaction of hate and anger is not surprising, and it is likely that in fact it was a more extensive sentiment than the figures indicate, since unquestionably many respondents, out of fear or politeness, did not reveal their sentiments with complete candor. Despite this factor, the frequency of hostile sentiments seems low. Two per cent of the respondents even volunteered the observation that they did not blame the U.S. for using the bomb. There is evidence that some hostility was turned against their own government, either before or after the surrender, although only a few said they wondered why their nation could not have made the bomb. In many instances the reaction was simply one of resignation. A common comment was, "Since it was war, it was just Shikata-ga-nai (Too bad)."

Admiration for the bomb was more frequently expressed than anger. Over one-fourth of the people in the target cities and surrounding area said they were impressed by its power and by the scientific skill which underlay its discovery and production.

Of greater significance are the reaction of the Japanese people as a whole. The two raids were all-Japan events and were intended so: the Allied powers were trying to break the fighting spirit of the Japanese people and their leaders, not just of the residents of Hiroshima and Nagasaki. Virtually all the Japanese people had a chance to react to the bomb, though the news had not reached to full spread at the time of the surrender. By the time the interviewing was done, only about two per cent of the population in rural areas and one per cent in the cities had not heard of the bomb.

The reactions found in the bombed cities appeared in the country as a whole -- fear and terror, anger and hatred against the users, admiration for the scientific achievement -- though in each case with less intensity. The effect of the bomb on attitudes toward the war in Japan as a whole was, however, much less marked than in the target cities. While 40% of the latter respondents reported defeatist feelings induced by the bomb, 28% of those in the islands as a whole attributed such reactions to the news of the bomb. There are at least three possible explanations of this difference. First, the level of confidence was quite low in Japan well before the time of the atomic bombing. Prior to 1 July 1945 doubts about a Japanese victory were felt by 74 per cent of the population. By the same data 47 per cent had become certain that a Japanese victory was impossible, and 34 per cent felt that they could not go on with the war. Under these circumstances, the announcement of a new and devastating weapon was merely an addition to the already eloquent evidence of national weakness. Second, the reaction of those at some distance from the target cities seems to have been blunted by their direct experience with other sorts of misfortunes and hardships, the common phenomenon of psychological distance increasing with geographical distance. In Japan as a whole, for example, military losses and failures, such as those at Saipan, the Phillippines, and Okinawa, were twice as important as this atomic bomb in inducing certainty of defeat. Other raids over Japan as a whole were more than three times as important in this respect. Consumer deprivations, such as food shortages and the attendant malnutrition, were also more important in bringing people to the point where they felt they could not go on with the war.

Third, the lack of understanding of the meaning of the new weapon in areas away from the target undoubtedly limited its demoralizing effect. As distance from the target cities increased, the effectiveness of the bombs in causing certainty of defeat declined progressively:

Group of Cities	% of Population certain of defeat because of Atomic Bomb
Hiroshima - Nagasaki	25%
Cities nearest to target cities.	23%
Cities near to target cities.	15%
Cities far from target cities.	8%
Cities farthest from target cities.	6%

Only in the nearest group of cities, within forty miles of Hiroshima or Nagasaki, was there a substantial effect on morale. Were the channels of mass communication as readily available to all the population as they are in the U.S. and had the use of the bomb received anything like the intensive coverage it had here, the effect on continued support of the war would probably have been greater. Something approaching such knowledge, of course, probably would have spread rather widely had

- 26 -

the war continued many more weeks, whether sanctioned by the censors or spread by the ever-active rumor channels so common in the country.

It is apparent that the effect of the atomic bombings on the confidence of the Japanese civilian population was remarkably localized. Outside of the target cities, it was subordinate to other demoralizing experiences. The effect which it did have was probably due largely to the number of casualties and the nature of the injuries received. These consequences were in part the result of surprise and the vulnerability of the raid defense system. Properly enforced warnings, precautions, and an emergency care organization of the scale of the bomb's effects might have reduced casualties and, therefore, the effects on morale.

Even in the target cities, it must be emphasized, the atomic bombs did not uniformly destroy the Japanese fighting spirit. Hiroshima and Nagasaki, when compared with other Japanese cities, were not more defeatist than the average. The bombs were tremendous personal catastrophes to the survivors, but neither time nor understanding of the revolutionary threat of the atomic bomb permitted them to see in these personal catastrophes a final blow to Japan's prospects for victory or negotiated peace.

3.   The Japanese Decision to Surrender.

The further question of the effects of the bombs on the morale of the Japanese leaders and their decision to abandon the war is tied up with other factors. The atomic bomb had more effect on the thinking of government leaders than on the morale of the rank and file of civilians outside of the target areas. It cannot be said, however, that the atomic bomb convinced the leaders who effected the peace of the necessity of surrender. The decision to surrender, influenced in part by knowledge of the low state of popular morale, had been taken at least as early as 26 June at a meeting of the Supreme War Guidance Council in the presence of the Emperor.

This decision did not, of course, represent the unanimous feeling of those influential in government circles. As early as the spring of 1944 a group of former prime ministers and others close to the Emperor had been making efforts toward bringing the war to an end. This group, including such men as Admiral Okada, Admiral Yonai, Prince Konoye, and Marquis Kido, had been influential in effecting Tojo's resignation and in making Admiral Suzuki Prime Minister after Koiso's fall. Even in the Suzuki cabinet, however, agreement was far from unanimous. The Navy Minister, Admiral Yonai, was sympathetic, but the War Minister, General Anami, usually represented the fight-to-the-end policy of the Army. In the Supreme War Guidance Council, a sort of inner cabinet, his adherence to that line was further assured by the participation of the Army and Navy Chiefs of Staff, so that on the peace issue this organization was evenly divided, with these three opposing the Prime

Minister, Foreign Minister, and Navy Minister. At any time military (especially Army) dissatisfaction with the Cabinet might have eventuated at least in its fall and possibly in the "liquidation" of the anti-war members.

Thus the problem facing the peace leaders in the government was to bring about a surrender despite the hesitation of the War Minister and the opposition of the Army and Navy Chiefs of Staff. This had to be done, moreover, without precipitating counter measures by the Army which would eliminate the entire peace group. This was done ultimately by bringing the Emperor actively into the decision to accept the Potsdam terms. So long as the Emperor openly supported such a policy and could be presented to the country as doing so, the military, which had fostered and lived on the idea of complete obedience to the Emperor, could not effectively rebel.

A preliminary step in this direction had been taken at the Imperial Conference on 26 June. At this meeting, the Emperor, taking an active part despite his custom to the contrary, stated that he desired the development of a plan to end the war as well as one to defend the home islands. This was followed by a renewal of earlier efforts to get the Soviet Union to intercede with the United States, which were effectively answered by the Potsdam Declaration on 26 July and the Russian declaration of war on 9 August.

The atomic bombings considerably speeded up these political maneuverings within the government. This in itself was partly a morale effect, since there is ample evidence that members of the Cabinet were worried by the prospect of further atomic bombings, especially on the remains of Tokyo. The bombs did not convince the military that defense of the home islands was impossible, if their behavior in government councils is adequate testimony. It did permit the Government to say, however, that no army without the weapon could possibly resist an enemy who had it, thus saving "face" for the Army leaders and not reflecting on the competence of Japanese industrialists or the valor of the Japanese soldier. In the Supreme War Guidance Council voting remained divided, with the War Minister and the two Chiefs of Staff unwilling to accept unconditional surrender. There seem little doubt, however, that the bombing of Hiroshima and Nagasaki weakened their inclination to oppose the peace group.

The peace effort culminated in an Imperial conference held on the night of 9 August and continued into the early hours of 10 August, for which the stage was set by the atomic bomb and the Russian war declaration. At this meeting the Emperor, again breaking his customary silence, stated specifically that he wanted acceptance of the Potsdam terms.

A quip was current in high government circles at this time that the atomic bomb was the real Kamikaze, since it saved Japan from further useless slaughter and destruction. It is apparent that in the atomic bomb the Japanese found the opportunity which they had been seeking, to break the existing deadlock within the government over acceptance of the Potsdam terms.

III. HOW THE ATOMIC BOMB WORKS

Out of the stories of Hiroshima and Nagasaki can be built up, detail by detail, the picture of how the atomic bomb works: the different forms of energy given off, the velocity and intensity of each, the sort of effects each has on animate and inanimate objects. In these factors is the real story of what happened at Hiroshima and Nagasaki, for in them chance circumstances are ruled out.

Spectators' accounts, whether of the New Mexico, the Hiroshima, or the Nagasaki explosion, describe similar pictures. At Nagasaki, for example, the bomb exploded at 1102 with a tremendous flash of blue-white light, like a giant magnesium flare. The flash was accompanied by a rush of heat and was followed by a huge pressure wave and the rumbling sound of the explosion. Curiously enough, this sound was not distinctly noted by those who survived near the center of the explosion, although it was heard as far as 15 miles away. People on the hillsides in the country at a considerable distance from Nagasaki told of seeing the blue-white and then multi-colored flash over the city, followed some seconds later by a tremendous clap, like thunder very close overhead. A huge snow-white cloud shot rapidly into the sky and the scene on the ground was obscured first by a bluish haze and then by a purple-brown cloud of dust and smoke.

The survivors were not aware at the time that a radically new bomb had been used. They were conscious of an explosion of tremendous power, but even the government had no conception, until President Truman's announcement was broadcast, of the new principle of operation. If we strip our minds of any lingering prejudice that the atomic bomb is supernatural or incomprehensible in its operation, we shall see why its uniqueness was not at first recognized.

1. The Nature of the Explosion

The atomic bomb works by explosion. An explosion is, in the words of the Smyth report, simply a "sudden and violent release of a large amount of energy in a small region." As do ordinary high explosives, atomic bombs release energy, though on an unprecedented scale. The energy takes three forms (one of which is new), and all the effects of the bomb can be referred directly to these three kinds of energy. They are:

(1) Heat (which is present in other explosions, as the familiar injuries known as "flash burns" on warships illustrate, but ordinarily not at high enough diffused temperatures to burn a man or set fire to combustible objects at any considerable distance from the explosion.)

(2).Radiation (similar to x-rays or to that from radium.)

(3) Blast or pressure (as from a demolition bomb.)

The whole discussion of the effects of the atomic bomb will be phrased in terms of these three kinds of energy. No other more mysterious or immeasurable forces acted; these were all.

These were enough. The energy released in atomic explosion is of such magnitude and from so concentrated a source that it sets entirely new problems in its use or in protection against it. Ordinary burning or explosion is a chemical reaction in which energy is released during the rearrangement of the atoms of the explosive material. In an atomic reaction, however, the identity of the atoms, not simply their arrangement, is changed. The change is more fundamental: in it, matter is transformed into energy. The energy released when a pound of nitroglycerine explodes, would, when converted into heat, raise the temperature of 150 pounds of water by 18° Fahrenheit. The explosion of a pound of uranium would produce an equal temperature rise in 2 billion pounds of water. Clearly, only a small part of the mass in the bomb's active core need be transformed to give an explosion of tremendous power.

At the time of the explosion, then, energy was given off in the forms of light, heat, gamma radiation, and pressure. The whole range of radiations, indeed, seems to have been present. There were heat radiations in the low frequency band below infra-red, visible waves of all colors (as the eyewitness accounts show), and penetrating radiations of very high frequency generally grouped as "gamma rays". Light and radiant heat ("flash heat") sped out in all directions at a rate of 186,000 miles per second, and the gamma rays at the same rate (though their effect was not immediately obvious.) The shock waves travelled much more slowly: it may be inferred from tests with high explosives that the rate at a relative short distance from the point of explosion was about two miles per second, and dropped rapidly to the speed of sound, or about one fifth of a mile per second. Thus the light, heat, and gamma radiation reached the target first, followed by shock and sound and the high winds of the blast.

(2) Heat

The center of the explosions--several hundred feet above ground--was a ball of fire. Because the radiant heat given off at the explosion easily charred combustible objects while ceasing so quickly that surfaces not in the direct line of radiation were unaffected, there are clearly marked "shadows" visible where objects were shielded against the heat. By projecting back the sharply defined outlines of these shadows, Japanese and Allied scientists have determined the height and diameter of the fireball. The two fireballs were apparently several hundred feet in diameter. The temperature at their core was virtually inconceivable--millions of degrees Centigrade. Even at its edge, the temperature was several thousand degrees; reasoning from the heat effects observed on human beings, bubbled roof tile, and combustible materials, Japanese and Allied scientists have placed the figure variously between 3000 and 9000° Centigrade. Energy given off in heat alone was estimated by Japanese physicists at the astronomical figure of 10^{13} calories.

The flash heat was intense enough to ~~cause~~ cause fires, despite the distance of the fire ball from the ground. Clothing ignited, though it could be quickly beaten out, telephone poles charred, thatched roofs of houses caught fire. In Hiroshima, the explosion started hundreds of fires almost simultaneously, the most distant of which was found 13,700 feet from ground zero; this, however, probably started when a building with a thatched roof collapsed onto a hot charcoal fire. Fires were started directly by flash heat in such easily ignitable substances as dark cloth, paper, or dry-rotted wood, within about 3,500 feet of ground zero; white-painted, concrete-faced or cement-stuccoed structures reflected the heat and did not ignite. A cedar bark roof and the top of a dry-rotted wooden platform 5200 feet west of ground zero, were reported to have been ignited by the bomb flash. The majority of initial fires in buildings, however, were started by secondary sources (kitchen charcoal fires, electric short-circuits, industrial process fires, etc.). In Nagasaki, both Japanese and American fire experts agreed that more fires were caused directly than indirectly, in a ratio of 60 to 40. The range of primary fire there is reported to have exceeded 10,000 feet.

Charred telephone poles were discernable for 10,000 feet south and 13,000 feet north of ground zero at Hiroshima, and for 13,000 feet or more at Nagasaki. Bubbling of roof tile occured at Hiroshima from ground zero out to 4000 feet, though with only scattered frequency after 2000 feet. The same phenomenon was reported at Nagasaki, accompanied again by scarring and peeling of granitic rocks, almost a mile from ground zero. A similar bubbled surface was obtained at the National Bureau of Standards by heating a ~~sample~~ sample of the tile to 1800° Centigrade for a period of four seconds. The effect so produced extended deeper into the tile than did the bubbling caused by the atomic bomb, which indicates that the explosion of the bomb subjected the tile to a temperature of more than 1800° for less than four seconds.

Persons reported feeling heat on their skin as far away as 24,000 feet. Burns of unprotected skin certainly occurred up to 12/13,000 feet, and reportedly up to 15,000 feet--nearly three miles. Serious or third-degree burns were suffered by those directly exposed within 4,500 feet, and occasionally as remote as 7,200 feet. In the immediate area of ground zero, the heat charred corpses beyond recognition.

Clothing as well as buildings afforded considerable protection against the flash. Even a clump of grass or tree leaf was on occasion adequate.

- 32 -

110

The implication clearly is that the duration of the flash was less than the time required for the grass or leaf to shrivel. While an accurate estimate is not possible, the duration could hardly have exceeded a fraction of a second.

3. Radiation

From the chain reaction which produced the mass release of energy in the explosion, a wide range of radiations were released. The light and heat are familiar elements of explosions, but the free neutrons and high-frequency radiations such as gamma rays are a new phenomenon. These radiations are highly penetrating and lethal.

The damaging penetration of radiation would be possible from three sources:

a.) From the high-frequency radiations, whether neutrons, gamma rays, or other unspecified rays, released in the chain reaction of the bomb.

b.) From lingering radio-activity from deposits of primary fission products scattered in the explosion.

c.) From induced radio-activity in the bombed area, caused by interaction of neutrons with matter penetrated.

Only the first cause seems to have had important effects, though there are detectable pockets of radio-activity in both cities. At Takasu, 10,000 feet from ground zero at Hiroshima, and at Nishi-yama, 6,500 feet from ground zero in Nagasaki, scientific measurements weeks after the explosion showed radioactivity. Presumably this was from deposits of primary fission products rather than induced radio-activity. In tests of the ground and bones of victims of radiation disease, certain substances--phosphorus, barium, strontium, rare earths--have shown radio-activity. Though evidence of lingering radio-activity is slight, it is strong enough to leave open the ominous possibility of a different situation had the bomb exploded at ground level.

The radiation apparently had no lasting effects on the soil or vegetation: seeds later planted within a few hundred feet of ground zero grew normally. Examination of sub-surface soil in the immediate area showed presence of earthworms and other life only a few inches below the surface. The effect on human procreation is as yet undetermined, but pregnant women within a mile of ground zero showed an increased number of miscarriages, and there was in most cases a low sperm count among men in the same area. Stories of harmful effects on people who came into the area after the explosion have been disproved by investigation.

The rays proved lethal for an average radius of 3000 feet

from ground zero. They caused loss of hair up to 7500 feet and occasionally beyond, andother mild effects up to almost two miles.

4. Blast

The pressure or shock wave travelled out in all directions from the explosion. The blast effects produced were uniform, and essentially those of conventional large high-explosive weapons though on a much larger scale. Thus, instead of localized effects such as the collapse of a roof truss or wall panel, entire buildings were crushed or distorted as units.

The blast pressure, as with high explosives, rose almost instantaneously to a peak, declined more slowly, and then fell below atmospheric pressure for a period about three times the period during which it was above atmospheric pressure. The positive period--that during which the pressure was greater than atmospheric--was of much greater peak pressure than the succeeding, or negative phase. Short though the positive phase was--probably only slightly longer than a second--it lasted longer than the positive phase of ordinary bombs. Thus the effect of the atomic bomb on buildings was usually that of a powerful push which shoved buildings over or left them leaning, whereas high explosive bombs strike sharply andmuch more briefly and tend to punch holes in walls. The durations was also long enough so that almost all building failures came during the positive phase. Comparatively few evidences were found of failures of members during the longer but less intense negative phase; window shutters blown outwards toward the explosion were very rare.

Experiments with high explosives have shown that the face-on peak pressures are approximately two to five times as intense as side-on peak pressures; thus greater damage was inflicted on walls or roofs facing the blast than on similar surfaces parallel to the blast. Near ground zero, the blast struck almost vertically downward. Buildings were crushed if weak, or the roofs were crushed in with little or no damage to the walls. Trunks of trees remained standing, but stripped of their branches; telephone poles, pushed over farther out, also remained errect near the center. Many small buildings were virtually engulfed in the pressure wave and simultaneously crushed from different directions. At somewhat greater distances, both horizontal and vertical components of the blast were appreciable, and buildings suffered damage both to roofs and to walls facing the explosion. At considerable distances, where the blast was travelling in an almost horizontal direction, damage was predominantly inflicted on walls during the blast. In such cases, the buildings were often completely racked by the inability of roof truss members to transmit the pressure to the far walls.

Shielding was more important at Nagasaki than at Hiroshima, because of the hills that divided the city. Building restrictions in

Japan after the 1923 earthquake limited building heights to 100 feet; thus there was little shielding by buildings from these air-burst bombs.

Reflection and diffraction effects were observed. Had the blast travelled in completely straight lines, more buildings would have survived in Nagasaki than actually did. Reflection effects were most clearly observed in the destruction of parapet walls of roofs on the side away from the bomb, where reflection of the blast wave from the roof reinforced the blast impinging on the wall directly. They were also visible in the displacing and cracking of concrete decks of bridges within one thousand feet of ground zero, where reflection of the blast wave from the water struck the bridges where their resistance was least.

The resistance of buildings depended very largely on their construction, as two examples show.

a.) In the area between two and three thousand feet from ground zero at Nagasaki, only 9.5 per cent of the floor area of reinforced concrete buildings was destroyed or structurally damaged. Yet in the ring between 4,000 and 5,000 feet from ground zero, 56 per cent of such buildings was destroyed or structurally damaged. Careful examination showed that the difference lay solely in design, construction detail, and materials: the bomb detonated over a section containing the most carefully and strongly built buildings in the city, the majority multi-story earthquake resistant structures. This strength more than compensated for the greater intensity of blast. A rapidly diminishing blast was capable of serious damage to weaker buildings further away, mostly high single-story industrial buildings, with thin shell-type arch roofs.

b.) At both cities, steel framed buildings with corrugated asbestos walls and roofs suffered less structural damage than those with corrugated iron or sheet metal walls and roofs. The corrugated asbestos crumbled easily, permitting the blast pressure to ~~aualize~~ equalize itself rapidly around the main framing members, but the steel siding transferred the pressure to the structural members, causing distortion or general collapse.

The limits of blast effects extended eight miles out, where some glass reportedly shattered in Hiroshima; at the same city, some roof stripping and disturbance of tiles was inflicted at the Japan Steel Company, 4.1 miles from ground zero.

In analyzing the extent of the destruction wrought by the bombs, it is necessary to discriminate between the two cities and between different types of buildings. Equivalent effects are found at Nagasaki over greater areas. Structural damage to reinforced concrete buildings, both earthquake resistant and non-earthquake resistant, occurred within an area of 0.05 square miles at Hiroshima, but at Nagasaki similar severe damage was inflicted in an area of 0.43 square miles.

Severe damage to one-story light steel frame buildings was equally extensive at the two cities; the area was 3.3 square miles at Nagasaki and 3.4 square miles at Hiroshima. Heavy steel frame buildings could be studied only at Nagasaki, where they suffered structural damage over an area of 1.8 square miles.

One-story brick buildings with load bearing walls were severely damaged within an area of 8.1 square miles at Nagasaki, and within an area of 6.0 square miles at Hiroshima. Multi-story brick buildings, which were studied only at Hiroshima, were severely damaged within an area of 3.6 square miles.

Wood domestic buildings were severely damaged within an area of 7.5 square miles at Nagasaki, and within an area of 6.0 square miles at Hiroshima. Wood frame industrial and commercial buildings, which were of inferior construction, were severely damaged within 9.9 square miles at Nagasaki, and 8.5 square miles at Hiroshima.

Maximum blast pressures fall off very rapidly as the distance from the detonation increases. In the two bombed cities, thus, reinforced concrete buildings of good construction were structurally damaged only when within a few hundred feet of ground zero. Indeed, ground zero itself was too distant from air zero for the earthquake-resistant buildings to be collapsed. It is the opinion of the Survey's engineers that at Hiroshima more thorough destruction near ground zero, without significant loss in the scope of destruction, could have been achieved had the bomb been detonated at a lower altitude.

5.   The Atomic Bomb Compared with Other Weapons.

In comparing the atomic bomb with other weapons, it is well to remember the importance of the height at which it exploded. Because of this distance from the targets, the atomic bombs did not exert at any point in Hiroshima or Nagasaki the high instantaneous peak pressures of even small high explosive bombs. For example, a single 100-pound bomb exploding at ground level exerts a higher blast pressure over an area of 1,000 square feet (for about 18 feet around its point of detonation) than did the atomic bomb at any point in either city.

114

That fact will place comparisons of the radii of effectiveness in the proper perspective. Even at the heights from which the atomic bomb was exploded in Japan, its blast effects were on a new scale because the duration of the blast was long compared to that of high explosive bombs. To take only one example: at Nagasaki brick buildings suffered structural damage within a radius averaging 6000 feet from ground zero. Comparable damage would be done by a 500-pound high explosive bomb burst at ground level for a radius of 55 feet; by a 1000-pound bomb for 80 feet; by a one-ton bomb for 110 feet; and by a two-ton bomb for 200 feet. A hypothetical ten-ton blockbuster (only ten-ton penetrating bombs have actually been used) could be expected to achieve equivalent damage over a radius of 400 feet. The area of effectiveness of the air-burst atomic bomb against brick buildings thus ranged from 15,000 times as great as that for a 500-pound bomb, to 225 times as great as that for the imaginary ten-ton blockbuster.

A simple table shows most strikingly the comparison between the striking forces needed for atomic and for conventional raids. Against the two atomic attacks can be set the data for the most effective single urban attack, that on Tokyo on 9 March 1945, and the average effort and results from the Twentieth Air Force's campaign against Japanese cities:

EFFORT AND RESULTS

	Hiroshima	Nagasaki	Tokyo	Average of 93 Urban Attacks
Planes	1	1	279	173
Bomb Load	1 atomic	1 atomic	1,667 tons	1,129 tons
Population Density per Square mile	46,000	65,000	130,000	unknown
Square miles destroyed	4.7	1.8	15.8	1.8
Killed and missing	70/80,000	35/40,000	83,600	1,850
Injured	70,000	40,000	102,000	1,830
Mortality rate per sq mile destroyed	15,000	20,000	5,300	1,000
Casualty rate per sq mile	32,000	43,000	11,800	2,000

What stands out from this compilation, even more than the extent of the destruction from a single concentrated source, is the unprecedented casualty rate from the combination of heat, blast, and gamma rays from the chain reaction.

On the basis of the known destructiveness of various bombs computed from the war in Europe and the Pacific and from tests, the Survey has estimated the striking force that would have been necessary to achieve the same destruction at Hiroshima and Nagasaki. To cause physical damage equivalent to that caused by the atomic bombs, approximately 1300 tons of bombs (one-fourth high explosives and three-fourths incendiaries) at Hiroshima and 600 tons (three-fourths high explosives and one-fourth incendiary) would have been required at Nagasaki--in the target area. To place that many bombs in the target area, assuming daylight attacks under essentially the same conditions of weather and enemy opposition that prevailed when the atomic bombs were dropped, it is estimated that 1600 tons of bombs would have had to be dropped at Hiroshima and 900 tons at Nagasaki. To these bomb loads would have had to be added a number of tons of anti-personnel fragmentation bombs to inflict comparable casualties; these would add about 500 tons at Hiroshima and 300 tons at Nagasaki. The total bomb loads would thus be 2100 tons at Hiroshima (400 HE, 1200 IB) and 1200 tons (675 HE, 225 IB) at Nagasaki. With each plane carrying ten tons, the attacking force required would have been 210 B-29s at Hiroshima and 120 B-29s at Nagasaki.

It should be kept in mind, however, that the area of damage at Nagasaki does not represent the full potential effectiveness of the atomic bomb used there. The damage was limited by the small size of the rather isolated section of the city over which the bomb exploded. Had the target been sufficiently large, with no sections protected by intervening hills, the area of damage would have been about five times as large. An equivalent bomb load which would correspond to the destructive power of the Nagasaki bomb rather than the imperfect results achieved would approximate 2200 tons of high explosives and incendiaries for physical damage plus 500 tons of fragmentation bombs for casualties, a total of 270 B-29 loads of ten tons each.

IV. SIGNPOSTS. The Danger, and What We Can Do About It.

A. The Danger.

The Survey's investigators, as they proceeded about their study, found an insistent question framing itself in their minds: "What if the target for the bomb had been an American city?" True, the primary mission of the Survey was to ascertain the facts just summarized. But conclusions as to the meaning of those facts, for citizens of the United States, forced themselves almost inescapably on the men who examined thoughtfully the remains of Hiroshima and Nagasaki. These conclusions have a different sort of validity from the measurable and ponderable facts of preceding sections, and therefore they are presented separately. They are not the least important part of this report, however, and they are stated with no less conviction.

No two cities, whether in Japan or the United States, are exactly alike. But the differences in terrain, layout and zoning, density, and type of construction can be allowed for one by one; when that is done, comparisons become possible. The most striking difference between American and Japanese cities is in residential districts: what happened to typical Japanese homes is not directly applicable to American residential districts. But in Japanese cities were many brick and wood frame buildings of Western or similar design and of good workmanship. It was the opinion of the Survey's engineers, with their professional familiarity with American buildings, that these Japanese buildings reacted to the bomb much as typical American buildings would have. And these buildings were exceedingly vulnerable: multi-story brick buildings with load-bearing walls were destroyed or seriously damaged over an area of 3.6 square miles at Hiroshima, while similar one-story brick buildings were destroyed or seriously damaged within an area of six square miles. Wood frame buildings built as industrial or commercial shops suffered similar damage in an area of over eight miles, while Japanese residences were destroyed or seriously damaged within an area of six square miles. This was at Hiroshima, where the less powerful bomb was used!

These figures indicate what would happen to typical wood, brick, and stucco structures in American cities. Modern reinforced concrete and steel frame buildings would fare better here -- as they did in Japan. But the following table shows how American cities are built, and how few are of blast-resistant construction.

117

CITY	TYPES OF STRUCTURES BY EXTERIOR MATERIAL (U.S. CITIES)					
	TOTAL STRUCTURES				OTHER	
	REPORTED	WOOD	BRICK	STUCCO	NUMBER	%
New York	591,319	236,879	299,482	41,661	13,297	2.2%
Washington	156,359	48,971	95,939	5,764	5,685	3.5%
Chicago	382,628	131,148	238,959	5,797	6,724	1.7%
Detroit	267,677	165,488	94,333	1,923	5,933	2.2%
San Francisco	105,180	61,172	2,334	40,902	722	0.7%

SOURCE: 16th Census of U.S. (1940) Vol. II.

The overwhelming bulk of the buildings in American cities could not stand up against an atomic bomb bursting a mile or a mile and a half from them.

And the people? We must not too readily discount the casualty rate because of the teeming populations of congested Japanese cities. American cities too have their crowded slums, and in addition tend to build vertically so that the density of the population is high in a given area even though each apartment dweller may have more living space than his Japanese equivalent.

POPULATION DENSITIES
U.S. AND JAPANESE CITIES

CITY	POPULATION	AREA SQ. MI.	POPULATION DENSITY PER SQ. MILE	
New York	7,492,000	322.8	23,200	
Manhattan (day)	3,200,000	22.2		145,000
Manhattan (night)	1,689,000	22.2		76,000
Bronx	1,493,700	41.4		34,000
Brooklyn	2,792,600	80.9		34,200
Queens	1,340,500	121.1		11,000
Staten Island	176,200	57.2		3,000
Washington	663,091	61.4	11,000	
Chicago	3,396,808	206.7	16,500	
Detroit	1,623,452	137.9	11,750	
San Francisco	634,536	44.6	14,250	
Hiroshima	340,000 (pre-war)	26.5	12,750	
Center of City	184,000 (1 Aug 45)	4.0	46,000	
Nagasaki	250,000 (pre-war)	35.	7,000	
Built-up area	220,000 (1 Aug 45)	3.4	65,000	

SOURCE: New York: Fortune, July, 1939 - Other U.S. cities: 16th Census of U.S. (1940)

Most of the population densities in this table are merely averages for people within a city limits. Most meaningful, therefore, are the figures for the central areas of Hiroshima and Nagasaki, and for the boroughs of New York. The casualty rates at Hiroshima and Nagasaki, applied to the massed inhabitants of Manhattan, Brooklyn, and the Bronx, yield a grim conclusion. These casualty rates, it must never be forgotten, result from the first atomic bombs to be used and from bombs burst at considerable distances above the ground. Improved bombs, perhaps detonated more effectively, may well prove still more deadly.

B. What We Can Do About It.

The danger is real — of that, the Survey's findings leave no doubt. Scattered through those findings, at the same time, are the clues to the measures that can be taken to cut down potential losses of lives and property. These measures must be taken or initiated now, if their cost is not to be prohibitive. But if a policy is laid down, well in advance of any crisis, it will enable timely decentralization of industrial and medical facilities, construction or blueprinting of shelters, and preparation for life-saving evacuation programs. The almost unprotected, completely surprised cities of Japan suffered maximum losses from atomic bomb attack. If we recognize in advance the possible danger and act to forestall it, we shall at worst suffer minimum casualties and disruption.

Since modern science can be marshalled for the defense as well as the attack, there is reason to hope that protective weapons and techniques will be improved. Even protective devices and vigilance, however, cannot be perfect guards against surprise or initial attack, or against the unlimited choices of targets offered an enemy through the range and speed of modern weapons. In our planning for the future, if we are realistic, we will prepare to minimize the destructiveness of such attacks, and so organize the economic and administrative life of the nation that no single or small group of successful attacks can paralyze the national organism. The foregoing description of the effectiveness of the atomic bomb has shown clearly that, despite its awesome power, it has limits of which wise planning will take prompt advantage.

Shelters

The most instructive fact at Nagasaki was the survival, even when near ground zero, of the few hundred people who were properly placed in the tunnel shelters. Carefully built shelters, though unoccupied, stood up well in both cities. Without question, shelters can protect those who get to them against anything but a direct hit. Adequate warning will assure that a maximum number get to shelters.

Analysis of the protection of survivors within a few hundred feet of ground zero shows that even gamma rays can be shielded against. At Hiroshima, for example, persons in a concrete building 3600 feet from ground zero showed no clinical effects from gamma radiation, but those protected only by wooden buildings at a similar distance suffered from radiation disease. The necessary thickness varies with the substance and with the distance from the point of detonation. Adequate shelters can be built which will reduce substantially the casualties from radiation.

Men arriving at Hiroshima and Nagasaki have been constantly impressed by the shells of reinforced concrete buildings still rising above the rubble of brick and stone or the ashes of wooden buildings. In most cases gutted by fire or stripped of partitions and interior trim, these buildings have a double lesson for us. They show, first, that it is possible without excessive expense to erect buildings which will satisfactorily protect their contents at distances of about 2000 feet or more from a bomb of the types so far employed. Construction of such buildings would be similar to earthquake resistant construction, which California experience indicates would cost about 10% to 15% more than conventional construction. Even against more powerful bombs or against near misses, such construction would diminish damage. Second, the internal damage illustrates the danger from interior details and construction which result in fire or flying debris in otherwise sound buildings. The elimination of combustible interiors and the provision of full-masonry partition walls, fire-resistive stair and elevator enclosures, and fire division walls would localize fires. Avoidance of glass, tile, or lath and plaster on wood stud would cut down damage from flying debris. The studies of the Physical Damage Division of the Survey support such recommendations and include many others.

The survival of sheltered sections of Nagasaki suggests forcefully the use that can be made of irregular terrain. Uneven ground reduces the spread and uniformity of blast effect. Terrain features such as rivers and parks afford natural firebreaks and avenues of escape.

Decentralization.

Hiroshima and Nagasaki were chosen as targets because of their concentration of activities and population. The population density of forty-five thousand or more per square mile of built-up area explains in part the high casualty rate. Significant therefore is the fact that deaths at Nagasaki, despite the greater population density, were only half those at Hiroshima: the difference can be assigned in the main to the separation of the dispersed built-up pockets at Nagasaki, in contrast to the uniform concentration of the inhabitants in the heart of Hiroshima. The Nagasaki bomb thus dissipated much of its energy against hills, water, or unoccupied areas, while the Hiroshima bomb achieved almost optimum effect.

The fate of industries in both cities again illustrates the value of decentralization. All major factories in Hiroshima were on the periphery of the city -- an escaped serious damage; at Nagasaki, plants and dockyards at the southern end of the city were merely intact, but those in the valley where the bomb exploded were seriously damaged. So spread out were the industries in both cities that no single bomb could have been significantly more effective than the two actually dropped.

Medical facilities, crowded into the heart of the city rather than evenly spread through it, were crippled or wiped out by the explosion. Only the previous removal of some stocks of medical supplies from Hiroshima to outlying communities, and the bringing in of aid, enabled the limited medical attention of the first few days.

These results underline those in conventional area raids in Germany, where frequently the heart of a city was devastated while peripheral industries continued to produce and where (particularly in Hamburg) destruction of medical facilities just at the time of greatest need hampered care of wounded.

The similar peril of American cities and the extent to which wise zoning has diminished it differ from city to city. Though a reshaping and partial dispersal of the national centers of activity are drastic and difficult measures, they represent a social and military ideal toward which very practical steps can be taken once the policy has been laid down. In the location of plants, administrative headquarters, and hospitals particularly, the value of decentralization is obvious, and can be obtained cheaply if the need is foreseen. For example, by wise selection of dispersed sites, the present hospital building program of the Veterans' Administration could be made to lessen our congestion without additional cost.

Reserve stocks of critical materials and of such products as medical supplies should be kept on hand. This principle of maintaining reserves applies also to the capital equipment of the country. Key producing areas must not be served by a single source of power or channel of transportation. Indispensable materials must not come from processing plants of barely adequate capacity. Production of essential manufactured goods -- civilian and military -- must not be confined to a few or to geographically centralized plants. And the various regions of the country should be encouraged to approach balanced economic development as closely as is naturally possible. An enemy viewing our national economy must not find bottlenecks which use of the atomic bomb could choke off to throttle our productive capacity.

Civilian Defense.

Because the scale of disaster would be certain to overwhelm the locality in which it occurs, mutual assistance organized on a national level is essential. Such national organization is by no means inconsistent with decentralization; indeed, it will be aided by the existence of the maximum number of nearly self-sustaining regions whose joint support it can coordinate. In addition, highly trained mobile units skilled in and equipped for fire-fighting, rescue work, and clearance and repair should be trained for an emergency which disrupts local organization and exceeds its capability for control.

Most important, a national civilian defense organization can prepare now the plans for necessary steps in case of crisis. Two complementary programs which should be worked out in advance are those for evacuation of unnecessary inhabitants from threatened urban areas, and for rapid erection of adequate shelters for people who must remain.

Active Defense.

Protective measures can substantially reduce the degree of devastation from an atomic bomb and the rate of casualties. Yet if the possibility of atomic attack on us is accepted, we must accept also the fact that no defensive measures alone can long protect us. At best they can minimize our losses and preserve the functioning of the national community through initial or continuing partial attack. Against full and sustained attacks they would be ineffectual palliatives.

As defensive weapons, atomic bombs are useful primarily as warnings as threats of retaliation which will restrain a potential aggressor from their use as from the use of poison gas or biological warfare. The mission of active defense, as of passive defense, is thus to prevent the surprise use of the atomic bomb from being decisive. A wise military establishment will make sure -- by dispersal, concealment, protection, and constant readiness of its forces -- that no single

122

blow or series of blows from an enemy can cripple its ability to strike back in the same way or to repel accompanying attacks from other air, ground, or sea forces. The measures to enable this un-relaxing state of readiness are not new; only their urgency is increased. Particularly is this true of the intelligence activities on which informed decisions and timely actions depend.

The need for research is not limited to atomic energy itself, but is equally important in propellants, detection devices, and other techniques of countering and of delivering atomic weapons. Also imperative is the testing of the weapon's potentialies under varying conditions. The coming Operations Crossroads, for example, will give valuable data for defining more precisely what is already known about the atomic bomb's effectiveness when air-burst; more valuable, however, will be tests under new conditions, to provide sure information about detonations at water level or underwater, as well as underground. While prediction of effects under differing conditions of detonation may have a high degree of probability, verified knowledge is a much better basis for military planning.

Conclusion.

One further measure of safety must accompany the others. To avoid destruction, the surest way is to avoid war. This was the Survey's recommendation after viewing the rubble of German cities, and it holds equally true whether one remembers the ashes of Hiroshima or considers the vulnerability of American cities.

Our national policy has consistently had as one of its basic principles the maintenance of peace. Based on our ideals of justice and of peaceful development of our resources, this disinterested policy has been reinforced by our clear lack of anything to gain from war -- even in victory. No more forceful arguments for peace and for the international machinery of peace than the sight of the devastation of Hiroshima and Nagasaki have ever been devised. As the developer and exploiter of this ominous weapon, our nation has a responsibility, which no American should shirk, to lead in establishing and implementing the international guarantees and controls which will prevent its future use.

This summary report was compiled from the special studies listed below, which contain the fully documented analysis of the Survey's technical experts. Inquiries concerning these reports should be addressed to the G-2 Section, U.S. Strategic Bombing Survey.

A. Physical Damage Division Report on Hiroshima.

    1. Object of Study
    2. Summary
    3. General Information
    4. Description of Target
    5. HE Attacks on Hiroshima
    6. Description of the Atomic Bomb Attacks
    7. Determination of Zero Points
    8. Typical Japanese Dwellings
    9. Fire: Cause and Extent
   10. Damage to Buildings
   11. Damage to Machine Tools
   12. Damage to Bridges
   13. Damage to Services and Utilities
   14. Damage to Stacks
   15. Probable Effects on Other Targets (Tentative)
   16. Photo Intelligence

B. Physical Damage Division Report on Nagasaki.

    1. Summary and General Information
    2. Industrial Buildings
    3. Public Buildings
    4. Utilities
    5. Machine Tools
    6. Bridges and Docks
    7. Fire
    8. Appendices

C. Medical Division Report: "Effects of the Atomic Bombings on the Public Health at Hiroshima and Nagasaki."

D. Urban Areas Division Reports on Hiroshima and Nagasaki.

E. Civilian Defense Division Reports on Japanese Civilian Defense.

F. Morale Division Report: "Effects on Morale of the Atomic Bombings of Hiroshima and Nagasaki".

G. Chairman's Office: "Japan's Decision to Surrender".

- 46 -

TOP SECRET

UNCLASSIFIED
CONFIDENTIAL

MEMORANDUM BY THE CHIEF OF STAFF, U. S. AIR FORCE

to the

SECRETARY OF DEFENSE

on

LONG RANGE DETECTION OF ATOMIC EXPLOSIONS

1. I believe that an atomic bomb has been detonated over the Asiatic land mass during the period 26 August 1949 to 29 August 1949. I base this on positive information that has been obtained from the system established by the U. S. Air Force for the long range detection of foreign atomic energy activities.

2. Fission products have been collected since 3 September 1949. Although the system is only partially developed, we have been fortunate in securing sufficiently large and fresh samples for effective scientific analysis. The cloud containing fission products was tracked by the U. S. Air Force from the Kamchatka peninsula to the vicinity of the British Isles where it was also picked up by the Royal Air Force.

3. Conclusions by our scientists based on physical and radio-chemical analyses of collected data have been confirmed by scientists of the AEC, United Kingdom and Office of Naval Research.

4. At my request, Dr. Vannevar Bush, Dr. J. Robert Oppenheimer, Dr. Robert Backer and Admiral William S. Parsons have reviewed our findings and concur unanimously in our conclusions.

5. The Joint Chiefs of Staff have been informed of the contents of this letter and the attached report.

read by
Mr Early
Mr Johnston
Mr Truman
21/Sept/49

J.M.S.
AFOAT.

Hoyt S. Vandenberg

TOP SECRET
CONFIDENTIAL
UNCLASSIFIED

125

UNCLASSIFIED

August 14, 1958

MEMORANDUM OF CONFERENCE WITH THE PRESIDENT
August 12, 1958

Others present: Chairman McCone
Admiral Foster
Dr. Teller
Dr. Bradbury
Mr. Gordon Gray
General Goodpaster

Admiral Foster introduced Drs. Teller and Bradbury, who were
to give a report to the President on the results of the atomic
tests of the Hardtack series. They showed sketches of each of
the weapons that had been tested, and summarized the results
achieved.

In further comment on the significance of a very small weapon
which had been fired, Dr. Teller indicated that there seems to be
tremendous potentiality in these very small devices -- even though
they consume a proportionately rather larger amount of plutonium
than do the larger weapons. He also made the point that, overall,
weapons as tested in the Hardtack series showed an improvement by
a [text deleted]

The President said that he hoped that if we find ourselves circum-
scribed on testing we still will be able to continue underground shots not
involving the release of fissionable products. He recognized that the
new thermonuclear weapons are tremendously powerful; however, they
are not, in many ways, as powerful as is world opinion today in ob-
liging the United States to follow certain lines of policy.

A. J. Goodpaster
Brigadier General, USA

UNCLASSIFIED

Documents on Nuclear Test Ban Negotiations

NEGOTIATIONS THAT ULTIMATELY LED TO THE LIMITED TEST BAN TREATY OF 1963 (SEE P.47-49) SPANNED OVER TWO U.S. PRESIDENTIAL ADMINISTRATIONS. THE FOLLOWING DOCUMENTS ARE SPEECHES, LETTERS AND PRESS STATEMENTS RELATING TO NUCLEAR TEST BAN NEGOTIATIONS FROM BOTH THE EISENHOWER AND KENNEDY ADMINISTRATIONS.

FOR RELEASE AT 2:00 P.M., EDT, AUGUST 22, 1958

James C. Hagerty, Press Secretary to the President

THE WHITE HOUSE

STATEMENT BY THE PRESIDENT

The United States welcomes the successful conclusion of the Geneva meeting of experts who have been considering whether and how nuclear weapons tests could be detected. Their conclusions indicate that, if there were an agreement to eliminate such tests, its effective supervision and enforcement would be technically possible.

This is a most important conclusion, the more so because it is concurred in by the experts of the Soviet Union. Progress in the field of disarmament agreements depends upon the ability to establish effective international controls and the willingness of the countries concerned to accept those controls. The fact therefore of an agreement on technical possibilities of inspection and control opens up a prospect of progress in the vitally important field of disarmament.

The United States, taking account of the Geneva conclusions, is prepared to proceed promptly to negotiate an agreement with other nations which have tested nuclear weapons for the suspension of nuclear weapons tests and the actual establishment of an international control system on the basis of the experts' report.

If this is accepted in principle by the other nations which have tested nuclear weapons, then in order to facilitate the detailed negotiations the United States is prepared, unless testing is resumed by the Soviet Union, to withhold further testing on its part of atomic and hydrogen weapons for a period of one year from the beginning of the negotiations.

As part of the agreement to be negotiated, and on a basis of reciprocity, the United States would be further prepared to suspend the testing of nuclear weapons on a year-by-year basis subject to a determination at the beginning of each year: (A) the agreed inspection system is installed and working effectively; and (B) satisfactory progress is being made in reaching agreement on and implementing major and substantial arms control measures such as the United States has long sought. The agreement should also deal with the problem of detonations for peaceful purposes, as distinct from weapons tests.

Our negotiators will be instructed and ready by October 31 this year to open negotiations with other similarly instructed negotiators.

As the United States has frequently made clear, the suspension of testing of atomic and hydrogen weapons is not, in itself, a measure of disarmament or a limitation of armament. An agreement in this respect is significant if it leads to other and more substantial agreements relating to limitation and reduction of fissionable material for weapons and to other essential phases of disarmament. It is in this hope that the United States makes this proposal.

128

# # # # #

UNCLASSIFIED

MEMORANDUM ON SOME TECHNICAL FACTORS INVOLVED IN POLICY DECISIONS ON ARMS LIMITATIONS AND SPECIFICALLY ON THE LIMITATION OF NUCLEAR TESTING

By J. R. Killian, Jr.

The recess of the Geneva Conference on the Discontinuance of Nuclear Tests with a stated date (April 13) for reconvening, requires the United States Government to re-examine its policy positions with respect to these negotiations.

This memorandum deals with my personal summary of the technical considerations which have a bearing on these policy questions. In discussing the technical factors, I recognize that they probably are of secondary importance to political and policy objectives.

Trends in Military Technology

Let me first point out how current trends in military technology emphasize the urgent importance of arms limitation of some kind. While deeply convinced that we must be unremittingly alert to keep ahead in our military technology, I also must conclude, in the light of factors mentioned below, that I see little opportunity to simplify the complexity of our military technology, to reduce the burden of defense, or to achieve a stable condition by means of military technology alone. On the contrary, the trend of technological measures and countermeasures will steadily complicate our defense, augment instability, and increase the cost of maintaining the relative strength we need.

We see this trend clearly revealed in our needs to make our strategic striking power, both aircraft and missiles, less vulnerable to surprise by dispersal, hardening, and shorter reaction times (including ground alert and possibly some degree of air alert). We see it clearly in the changing require-

UNCLASSIFIED

ments of air and missile defense as typified by the problems associated with
the Sage system and Bomarc, with Nike-Zeus, ballistic missile early warning systems, antisubmarine warfare systems, and with requirements for
more comprehensive communications systems.

We see further evidence in the effort to improve the yield-to-weight
ratio of atomic weapons, and in the developing program for using space and
space vehicles for military purposes. The possibilities for military technology in modifying the geophysical environment of the earth are illustrated
in the possibilities (remote) now envisaged for weather modification and by
the results of Argus and other high-altitude experiments.

As military technology moves toward more systems operating on a
global scale, and as it begins to make use of extraterrestrial space and
effects, and as the time-scale becomes more condensed, we face the requirement for weapons systems, offensive and defensive, of increasing performance
and complexity. Because of rapid technological change, we see the new
systems overlapping with quickly obsolescing older ones and we see the
consequent possibilities of systems being piled upon systems.

As complexity increases, the chances for error or aberrations on the
part of humans and machines grow greater, and the consequences of such
errors and aberrations (e.g., accidental war) become enormous. The
shortened time-scale also reduces the opportunity for careful judgment by
increasing the rewards for spontaneous response.

130

The overriding technological fact, however, is the continued build-up of improved high-performance nuclear weapons on both sides to make possible catastrophic effects if they are used in massive attacks.

Another technical factor involving uncertainties is the problem of fallout. The biological effects of radiation involve uncertainties, particularly in the genetic area, and we may possibly face a growing body of sober scientific judgment that the fallout hazard is greater than we now believe.

The profound over-all effect of these trends points to the great urgency and importance of our diligently and creatively seeking methods of arms limitation--limitation which will not weaken our position relative to the Soviets.

Some Technical Aspects of Arms Limitation

If progress is to be made in any kind of arms limitation (such as reducing the hazard of surprise attack or limiting the production of fissionable material or any other form of limitation), the agreements for such limitation will have to be accompanied by some form of monitoring to assure both sides that agreements are being carried out. We have so far held steadfastly to the principle that arms limitations agreements must be monitored. If we are to achieve such agreements and preserve this principle, then we will certainly be faced with the design of monitoring and inspection systems that will have to fulfill technical, military and political requirements.

While the discontinuance or limitation of nuclear tests are not, except in a limited way, disarmament measures, they do have a special importance

in establishing the principle and techniques and practice of monitoring agreements. On the technical side, and perhaps on the military and political sides too, we have given more study and thought to monitoring and inspection systems for the control of nuclear tests than we have for any aspect of arms limitation. We probably have a better chance for arriving at some acceptable arrangement for monitoring and inspection of nuclear tests than we have for any other form of arms limitation. This was illustrated by the difficulties encountered in the Geneva Conference on Surprise Attack. A monitoring and inspection system for nuclear tests is likely to be simpler and more achievable than a monitoring and inspection system for surprise attack. We are not only further advanced in the technical aspects of the problem, but we have large pressures of world opinion favoring the achievement of such an agreement.

What Do We Do About the Geneva Negotiations?

Let me now turn specifically to the problems associated with our negotiations on the limitation or discontinuance of nuclear tests. We must recognize that new data secured in the Hardtack II tests, together with conclusions reached in recent studies on underground testing and on testing in outer space, leave us in a position where the system agreed to last summer at the Conference of Experts involves more substantial and significant uncertainties than believed at the time. While the Panel on Seismic Improvement has concluded that the Geneva system can be substantially restored to its

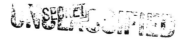

originally-conceived capability, they also concluded that by deliberate concealment it would be possible to reduce the signal from an underground explosion by a factor of 10 or more and that, in theory at least, the signal might be reduced by a much larger factor than this. It is, therefore, impossible--without further tests--to give any firm estimate of the capability of the Geneva system for underground tests. This does not mean that such a firm estimate may not be achievable in the foreseeable future.

The Panel on High Altitude Detection indicated the technical feasibility of testing in outer space, as well as the technical feasibility of a system to detect these tests. Such a system would have a detection threshold which would be as high as a few hundred kilotons if the violator of the agreement resorted to very expensive measures to try to achieve concealment.

The reports of these two panels represent as good a discussion of the technical possibilities as could be achieved in the time available. They emphasize that continuing studies and experiments on a reasonable scale are needed for the further understanding of test detection and for the understanding of concealment possibilities. It was clear from the findings of both panels that attempts to conceal tests, either underground or in outer space, would be very costly.

The Concept of Probability or Calculated Risk

In our policy-making, we should recognize that no technological system is going to be perfect or absolute in its performance. We must consider the effect of such technological inspection systems in terms of probability and

consider their restraining value on the basis of an estimated probability
to detect within stipulated limits.

In a world of rapidly-changing technology, it may be impossible to
devise fool-proof monitoring systems--either for nuclear test cessation
or for other forms of agreed arms limitation. The most that these systems
may accomplish will be to make evasion very costly and very uncertain.
These may be the principal functions of monitoring systems. Hence, if
they are to be of maximum use to us, they would have to be supplemented
by highly-developed intelligence systems of our own and with appropriate
military measures.

Political-Technical Factors in Geneva Negotiations

The current Geneva negotiations indicate that there are very great
difficulties in reaching a satisfactory agreement with the Soviets on the
critical questions of voting, staffing, and inspection. The present Soviet
position on these questions is clearly unacceptable since it would eliminate
even the deterrent effect of the Geneva System. We should not seek to find
our way out of the present impasse in Geneva by relaxing our requirements
on the critical political aspects of the control organization.

It would, therefore, seem desirable at this stage to draw back from
our original efforts to achieve a system as comprehensive as that discussed
by the Geneva Conference of Experts last summer and to settle for some
more limited form of test agreement that would simplify both the technical
and political requirements of the control organization. The most obvious

possible alternative approach would be to seek an agreement which would provide for no testing in the atmosphere but would permit testing underground and at high altitudes. The timing and method of introducing this alternative is not dealt with here.

It would seem important that if we seek to agree to exclude atmospheric testing that we propose doing so by formal agreement (rather than by unilateral action) which involves some system of monitoring and which thus preserves the principle of monitoring and, perhaps, inspection and provides experience with such a system.

Such an agreement migh include specific provisions for a phased, evolutionary extension of the test ban to include coverage of testing underground and at high altitudes when controls adequate to detect such tests become technically available. Research to develop this more extensive control organization might well be made a responsibility of the control organization itself.

If our decision is to proceed in this direction, it is important that we make an early technical analysis to determine what we mean by the "atmosphere." In view of the present discussion about fallout from the stratosphere, it seems clear that a system to limit testing to the troposphere will neither solve the fallout problem nor alleviate public concern about this problem. Some radioactivity will return to earth from tests conducted out to a distance of many thousands of miles. The limit of the "atmosphere" will probably be difficult to establish.

It is also possible that an agreement not to test in the atmosphere might be accompanied by an agreement to conduct explosions in outer space only under internationally-supervised conditions, or alternatively, it is possible to define somewhat sharply the outer limits of the atmosphere and assume that unilaterally-planned testing will take place beyond that altitude. There are other kinds of technical problems that would need to be resolved, such as the conduct of explosions lightly covered with earth, or explosions under water.

It is reasonably certain, however, that these technical matters can be satisfactorily resolved from the U.S. point of view and that it would be possible to suggest a monitoring system that would be relatively simple and that would greatly reduce, if not eliminate, the requirement for inspection teams and the fear that they would be used for purposes of espionage.

However, before proposing such an agreement, I believe we should know, more clearly than we do now, the effect of this type of agreement on our own weapons program. Specifically, estimates should be made as to the additional costs involved and the usefulness of data obtained if our test program were to continue at its present rate and all tests were conducted either underground or in outer space. In addition, we should examine carefully the effect of an atmosphere test ban on our anti-intercontinental ballistic missile weapon system testing.

Sustained Disarmament Studies

The complexities inherent in understanding the monitoring of arms limitation agreements and the great importance of our achieving a thorough understanding of what is to our advantage or disadvantage suggest the importance to the United States of undertaking systematic and sustained studies of the technical, military, and political aspects of arms limitation. Our experience in the Geneva Conference on Reducing the Hazards of Surprise Attack pointed up the deficiencies of ad hoc and hurried preparation for such negotiations.

Even though an agreement for limited nuclear test cessation remains our first goal, we should look beyond this. We might well direct our studies and planning toward a possible reduction in the advanced means of <u>delivery</u> of nuclear weapons. This may be a more practical objective than control of nuclear weapons stockpiles and production.

A small but important beginning was made in this direction by the Geneva Conference on Surprise Attack. The failure of this conference should not deter further efforts. It seems especially urgent that we proceed with further studies of ways to reduce the hazards of surprise attack.

We must also undertake studies and experiments to improve our capacity to detect tests other than in the atmosphere (as, for example, in outer space), even if we achieve no agreements. The research and experiments recommended by the Panel on Seismic Improvement and the Panel on High Altitude Detection should be carefully considered and followed up as a part of our long-term effort to advance the technology of detection.

Summary

The trends in military technology, together with the threat of catastrophic war, in the continuing development of nuclear weapons systems emphasize the overwhelming importance of seeking sound ways of limiting armaments. The possibilities of uncertainties in scientific estimates of biological effects of radiation hazards should be kept in mind in formulating policy.

Since any kind of arms limitation will probably have to be accompanied by a monitoring system, it is important to establish the principle of monitoring and inspection and to achieve an agreement which will give us experience in monitoring. The monitoring of nuclear tests has received more study and is more thoroughly understood than any other arms limitation monitoring. This is an added reason for seeking an agreement for the limitation of atomic tests.

It would seem technically feasible to achieve a sound agreement that would involve the stoppage of tests in the atmosphere, this stoppage to be subject to monitoring through an agreement. Such an agreement might provide for the evolutionary development of improved detection systems for underground and outer-space testing. If we are to seek this kind of modified test limitation agreement, we should at once clarify the technical premises for such an agreement.

We also need to organize and pursue on a sustained basis creative efforts to understand the technical, military, and political aspects of arms limitation of other kinds than nuclear tests cessation.

3/30/59

TO THE SENATE OF THE UNITED STATES:

With a view to receiving the advice and consent of the Senate to ratification, I transmit herewith a certified copy of the Treaty banning nuclear weapon tests in the atmosphere, in outer space and underwater, signed at Moscow òn August 5, 1963, on behalf of the United States of America, the United Kingdom of Great Britain and Northern Ireland, and the Union of Soviet Socialist Republics.

This Treaty is the first concrete result of eighteen years of effort by the United States to impose limits on the nuclear arms race. There is hope that it may lead to further measures to arrest and control the dangerous competition for increasingly destructive weapons.

The provisions of the Treaty are explained in the report of the Acting Secretary of State, transmitted herewith. Essentially it prohibits only those nuclear tests that we ourselves can police. It permits nuclear tests and explosions underground so long as all fallout is contained within the country where the test or explosion is conducted.

In the weeks before and after the Test Ban Negotiations, the hopes of the world have been focused on this Treaty. Especially in America, where nuclear energy was first unlocked, where the danger of nuclear war and the meaning of radioactive fallout are so clearly recognized, there has been understanding and support for this effort.

139

Now the Treaty comes before the Senate, for that careful study which is the constitutional obligation of the members of that body. As that study begins I wish to urge that the following considerations be kept clearly in mind:

First: This Treaty is the whole agreement. United States negotiators in Moscow were instructed not to make this agreement conditioned upon any other understanding; and they made none. The Treaty speaks for itself.

Second: This Treaty advances, though it does not assure, world peace; and it will inhibit, though it does not prohibit, the nuclear arms race.

-- While it does not prohibit the United States and the Soviet Union from engaging in all nuclear tests, it will radically limit the testing in which both nations would otherwise engage.

-- While it will not halt the production or reduce the existing stockpiles of nuclear weapons, it is a first step toward limiting the nuclear arms race.

-- While it will not end the threat of nuclear war or outlaw the use of nuclear weapons, it can reduce world tensions, open a way to further agreements and thereby help to ease the threat of war.

-- While it cannot wholly prevent the spread of nuclear arms to nations not now possessing them, it prohibits assistance to testing in these environments by others; it will be signed by many other potential testers; and it is thus an important opening wedge in our effort to "get the genie back in the bottle."

Third: The Treaty will curb the pollution of our atmosphere.
While it does not assure the world that it will be forever free from
the fears and dangers of radioactive fallout from atmospheric tests,
it will greatly reduce the numbers and dangers of such tests.

Fourth: This Treaty protects our rights in the future. It cannot
be amended without the consent of the United States, including the
consent of the Senate; and any party to the Treaty has the right to
withdraw, upon three months' notice, if it decides that extraordinary
events related to the subject matter of the Treaty have jeopardized
its supreme interests.

Fifth: This Treaty does not alter the status of unrecognized
regimes. The provisions relating to ratification by others, and the
precedents of international law, make it clear that our adherence to
this Treaty, and the adherence of any other party, can in no way
accord or even imply recognition by the United States or any other
nation of any regime which is not now accorded such recognition.

Sixth: This Treaty does not halt American nuclear progress.
The United States has more experience in underground testing than
any other nation; and we intend to use this capacity to maintain the
adequacy of our arsenal. Our atomic laboratories will maintain an
active development program, including underground testing, and
we will be ready to resume testing in the atmosphere if necessary.
Continued research on developing the peaceful uses of atomic
energy will be possible through underground testing.

Seventh: This Treaty is not a substitute for, and does not diminish the need for, continued Western and American military strength to meet all contingencies. It will not prevent us from building all the strength that we need; and it is not a justification for unilaterally cutting our defensive strength at this time. Our choice is not between a limited Treaty and effective strategic strength -- we need and can have both. The continuous build-up in the power and invulnerability of our nuclear arsenal in recent years has been an important factor in persuading others that the time for a limitation has arrived.

Eighth: This Treaty will assure the security of the United States better than continued unlimited testing on both sides. According to a comprehensive report prepared by the responsible agencies of government for the National Security Council, the tests conducted by both the Soviet Union and the United States since President Eisenhower first proposed this kind of treaty in 1959 have not resulted in any substantial alteration in the strategic balance. In 1959 our relative nuclear position was strong enough to make a limited test ban desirable, and it remains so today. Under this Treaty any gains in nuclear strength and knowledge which could be made by the tests of any other power -- including not only underground tests but even any illegal tests which might escape detection -- could not be sufficient to offset the ability of our strategic forces to deter or survive a nuclear attack and to penetrate and destroy an aggressor's homeland. We have, and under this Treaty we will continue to have, the nuclear strength that we need. On the other hand, unrestricted testing -- by which other powers could develop all kinds of weapons through atmospheric tests more cheaply and quickly than they could underground -- might well lead to a weakening of our security. It is true that the United States would be able to make further progress if atmospheric tests were continued -- but so would the Soviet Union and, indeed, so could other nations. It should be remembered that only one atomic test was required to complete the development of the Hiroshima bomb. Clearly the security of the United States -- the security of all mankind -- is increased if such tests are prohibited.

Ninth: <u>The risks in clandestine violations under this Treaty are far smaller than the risks in unlimited testing.</u> Underground tests will still be available for weapons development; and other tests, to be significant, must run substantial risks of detection. No nation tempted to violate the Treaty can be certain that an attempted violation will go undetected, given the many means of detecting nuclear explosions. The risks of detection outweigh the potential gains from violation, and the risk to the United States from such violation is outweighed by the risk of a continued unlimited nuclear arms race. There is further assurance against clandestine testing in our ability to develop and deploy additional means of detection, in our determination to maintain our own arsenal through underground tests, and in our readiness to resume atmospheric testing if the actions of others so require.

Tenth: This Treaty is the product of the steady effort of the United States Government in two Administrations, and its principles have had the explicit support of both great political parties. It grows out of the proposal made by President Eisenhower in 1959 and the Resolution passed by the Senate in that same year; and it carries out the explicit pledges contained in the Platforms of both parties in 1960. Nothing has happened since then to alter its importance to our security. It is also consistent with the proposals this Administration put forward in 1961 and 1962 -- and with the Resolution introduced in the Senate, with wide bipartisan support, in May of 1963.

This Treaty is in our national interest. While experience teaches us to be cautious in our expectations and ever-vigilant in our preparations, there is no reason to oppose this hopeful step. It is rarely possible to recapture missed opportunities to achieve a more secure and peaceful world. To govern is to choose; and it is my judgment that the United States should move swiftly to make the most of the present opportunity and approve the pending Treaty. I strongly recommend that the Senate of the United States advise and consent to its ratification.

THE WHITE HOUSE,

August 8, 1963.

FEDERAL CIVIL DEFENSE ADMINISTRATION

Fallout is nothing more than particles of matter in the air, made radioactive by nuclear or thermonuclear explosions. When an atomic or hydrogen bomb is exploded close to the ground, thousands of tons of atomized earth, building materials, rocks, and gases are sucked upward, sometimes to a height of 80,000 feet or more. They help form the mushroom cloud which is always seen with one of these explosions.

Some of these radioactive particles spill out in the immediate area of the explosion soon after it occurs, but others may be carried by the upper winds for many miles. Sooner or later, however, they settle to earth. This is called fallout.

RADIOACTIVITY
IS NOTHING NEW...

THE WHOLE WORLD IS RADIOACTIVE

But normal amounts are not dangerous. It is only when radioactivity is present in highly concentrated amounts, such as those created by atomic and hydrogen bomb explosions, that it becomes dangerous. Radioactive fallout is sometimes highly concentrated.

If you are exposed to it long enough—

IT WILL HURT YOU!

IT MAY EVEN KILL YOU!

WHOM WILL IT HIT ?
IT COULD HIT YOU !

WHO ME ?

Yes, it could settle anywhere. The upper winds could carry fallout to the most remote parts of the country. Small towns and rural areas many miles from the scene of a nuclear explosion may be endangered by fallout. Every citizen is a potential target for fallout.

Civil Defense officials and weather experts will estimate the probable path and speed of approaching fall-out and keep you posted.

Tune your AM radio to 640 or 1240 kilocycles, your Conelrad stations, for official Civil-Defense news and instructions.

HERE'S HOW YOU'LL KNOW IT

Civil Defense radiological monitoring teams will detect fallout if it is present in your area. They will tell you when it is safe and when you must take protective measures.

149

IF IT COMES MY WAY, WHAT DO I DO THEN?

An ordinary frame-house will offer some protection. It may cut radiation danger by about one-half. Get on the floor, away from doors and windows, or preferably go to a location with additional walls at the center of the house.

If there is enough warning time, your local Civil Defense director may order a general evacuation of the area to get away from the bomb or its effects, before it hits.

A basement shelter will offer even more protection. The radiation danger there might be one-tenth as bad.

IF YOU DON'T HAVE TIME TO EVACUATE, SEEK THE BEST AVAILABLE SHELTER

An underground shelter with 3 feet of earth above it will give you almost complete protection if it is equipped with a door and an air filter.

150

An old-fashioned storm-cellar or root cellar is ideal. Stock it with food staples as Grandmother did, and water supplies, first-aid kits, blankets, a lantern, fuel . . .

DON'T GET DISCOURAGED

EVERYTHING YOU NEED TO LIVE IN IT FOR A FEW DAYS

DON'T GET PANICKY

FOLLOW THESE SIMPLE RULES

Prepare a shelter area in your home or backyard, whether you live in a city or in the country.

Stock your shelter with a day supply of emergency food and water.

Get a radio, preferably battery-operated, and keep it in a safe place. Mark the Conelrad frequencies. Civil Defense news and instructions will be provided at these frequencies.

If you think you have been in a serious fallout area, remove your outer clothing and wash the exposed parts of your body thoroughly. Unless you have been subjected to serious contamination, it may not be necessary to destroy or discard the clothing, since it can be made safe by laundering or by simply waiting for the radioactivity to decay.

152

TO SUM IT UP...

Americans are hard to scare. Of course, we are worried about the forces science has unlocked. We would not be intelligent human beings otherwise.

But this problem can be solved—as others have been—by American ingenuity and careful preparation—

NOW

See your local Civil Defense office

TODAY

Let Civil Defense help you to help yourself and the Nation, to be prepared.

U. S. GOVERNMENT PRINTING OFFICE 1956 O - 337755

Research and Reference Service

WORLDWIDE REACTION TO COMMUNIST CHINA'S
THIRD NUCLEAR EXPLOSION

R-87-66

May 12, 1966

This is a research report, not a statement of Agency policy

HIGHLIGHTS

Prominent and attentive news coverage was given Communist China's third nuclear explosion in the world press, followed by considerable editorial discussion. Peking's Asian neighbors accounted for a high volume of editorial comment. Latin Americans, sensitized by France's upcoming tests in the Pacific, voiced anxiety at developments.

The news out of Peking was generally seen as bad. A mood of concern generally marked comment around the world, as editors stressed the view that Communist China posed a growing threat to peace by her rapid emergence as a nuclear power. Although it was pointed out that the immediate military significance of the event was limited by the fact that Peking as yet has no effective delivery system for its nuclear devices, there was little disposition to dismiss the achievement on this ground. A widespread belief that Red China had made a dramatic and sensational nuclear "leap forward" intensified impact and the feeling that "time was running out." Dangers of nuclear proliferation were frequently stressed.

Communist China's motives were variously assessed as ambition to enter the nuclear club posthaste, to recoup losses in esteem among the Afro-Asian nations, to intimidate dissident homefront elements, and to "upset the equilibrium of fear" resulting from the current U.S. and Soviet nuclear stalemate. There was little expectation that Peking would respond favorably to Western (or Soviet) overtures in the field of non-proliferation or nuclear disarmament.

Many commentators continued to urge, however, that Peking be brought into the U.N. and the "community of nations." Others, deploring the folly of the arms race, urged that the nuclear nations, especially the U.S. and the USSR, act urgently now to forge the machinery for effective cooperation in nuclear control. The U.S. was often advised to end its "isolation of China."

Regional or national concerns emerged early in comment. Indian papers debated whether India should make its own bomb.

i

Japanese writers and experts were preoccupied with supposed immediate peril to Japan. Various countries were cited as presumably spurred by the Chinese example to become nuclear powers.

Soviet media did not react except in brief and non-committal notation of the event. Czechoslovakia and Yugoslavia condemned the test and Albania hailed its Asian ally's achievement.

CONTENTS

ii

The Far East news media treated Communist China's third nuclear detonation as an event of the highest significance. Japanese media, in particular, reacted swiftly with heavy coverage, background material in depth, and extensive editorial analyses. Leading newspapers in the capital cities of Taipei, Manila, Seoul, Saigon and Kuala Lumpur prominently featured wire service reports and exclusive stories on the test-explosion and accorded it moderate editorial attention.

Most Far East commentators voiced widespread apprehension, distrust, condemnation and protest over Peking's unilateral nuclear action, which many considered to be in defiance of prevalent world opinion. There was a broad consensus that Communist China's nuclear coming-of-age, as evidenced by the latest test, represented a three-pronged military-political-psychological threat. Few, however, foresaw precisely the form it would take.

Japanese press opinion was preoccupied with Japan's own peril and security in light of Peking's nuclear capacity, and in vague terms stressed the need for immediate disarmament measures. Most Tokyo newspapers noted the quick tempo with which Communist China had entered the nuclear age and the attendant political and psychological ramifications for neighboring Asian nations. Commentators found little comfort in Peking's pledge not to trigger a nuclear conflict. They likewise shared an overriding fear of nuclear proliferation.

Cutting across the area as a whole, editorials amplified four other salient points: (1) that Peking's latest test would aggravate the cold war confrontation between the United States and Communist China, (2) that it would harden policy lines on both sides and impede a peaceful settlement, (3) that it might result in even greater isolation of the Peking regime, and (4) that it could produce economic repercussions in Communist China. Editorials from Japan, Malaysia and Burma failed to see eye-to-eye on whether Peking's current nuclear accomplishment would upset the existing U.S.-Soviet monopoly and balance in the nuclear field.

Peking's Nuclear Coming-of-Age

Assessment of the nuclear bomb feat itself and its technical potential drew a mixed response. At one extreme, the <u>Guardian</u> (Burma) credited China with having "blasted the 'balance of terror' the nuclear powers of the West have hitherto held" and predicted that "Peking now has the know-how, if not the capability yet -- which she will acquire in the course of not many years -- to retaliate massively in nuclear war."

1

Sankei (Japan) conceded that "the recent success in the A-test has given Peking a lift in prestige and has elevated its position as a nuclear power." In Kuala Lumpur, the Straits Times (Malaysia) resigned itself to the eventuality of Peking's arrival as an advanced nuclear power "whether great powers like it or not, in no more than a decade and perhaps less."

At the other extreme, Tokyo Shimbun's (Japan) "Fusei" column glossed over the Chinese H-bomb as "a mere firecracker" with no delivery system. Kuala Lumpur's Berita Harian (Malaysia) considered the present stage of Chinese development "too primitive to threaten us," while the South China Morning Post (Hong Kong) thought it represented "scarcely more than an enormously expensive propaganda gesture." Mainichi's (Japan) analysis noted that "it may take 20-30 years for China to reach the scientific standards of a formidable power" with real "nuclear fangs" to counter the "imperialist camp."

Peking's Pledge Doubted

Peking's pledge not to trigger the first nuclear strike failed to alleviate the apprehensions of Tokyo, Kuala Lumpur and Hong Kong commentators. Mainichi, for example, said: "This is no assurance for Japan, inasmuch as no nuclear power has announced it would strike first." Sankei (Japan) shared the same distrust: "When you think of the abnormal efforts Peking has put in the development of nuclear weapons and of its revolutionary principles, you can never trust its words." In the same vein, Berita Harian had this to say: "Even though she claimed the H-bomb would not be used in any nuclear war, the world is not convinced she would not use it for aggressive purposes. In other words, Peking will not hesitate to harass other nations and will not even hesitate to destroy the world."

On the other hand, the Guardian expressed reassurance that China "would not under any circumstance be the first to employ nuclear weapons, although it might not put all those striving for world peace quite completely at ease." The Malay Mail, while placing little credence in the "goulash" theory of Communist China becoming less bellicose when it has its own nuclear arsenal declared that "the clear need exists to attempt to talk Communist China out of its arrogant isolation and back into the community of nations."

Nuclear Disarmament

Fearful of Peking's nascent nuclear might, editorials areawide dwelled on the themes of nuclear disarmament, a total nuclear ban, nuclear proliferation, and world peace. Atomic-sensitive Japan was logically the most vociferous in this regard.

2

Asahi, for instance, called for "supra-partisan national diplomacy" for the "positive promotion of world nuclear disarmament," while Yomiuri typically urged the United States and Soviet Union to make "earnest efforts to realize the prevention of nuclear proliferation and a total ban on nuclear tests as well as to assume the initiative in convening a world disarmament conference with the participation of Communist China."

In Malaysia, the Straits Times declared that "the danger of proliferation grows" and warned that "in another year or two, the opportunity of any treaty at all virtually will have disappeared." In South Korea, the Chosun Ilbo declared that "Communist China is inciting the spread of nuclear weapons and is flagrantly opposing the worldwide disarmament effort." In Burma, the Guardian warned that "The time has come for the urgent task of outlawing nuclear weapons." And in Taipei, Hsin Sheng Poh concluded that "The danger Peking's third nuclear explosion poses for world peace and the security of millions of living souls is a matter that defies description."

Political and Psychological Impact

A number of editorials focused on the political ramifications in the wake of the test. Most of these subscribed to the belief that the latest bomb would have a profound effect on the international scene. Nihon Keizai (Japan), for example, feared Peking's international diplomacy would become "firm" in the future, whereas Tieng Vang (South Vietnam) claimed China's new device "will only make the USSR adopt a more rigid attitude toward Peking." Asahi reasoned "Peking probably intends to use its developing nuclear weapons capacity to drive a wedge between other powers and to increase psychological and political impact on its neighbors." Some editorials suggested that the bomb would be used to support national liberation struggles and to gain Peking the leadership in Asia. And others, such as Mainichi, expected that Peking intended "to blackmail Japan and SEATO nations and seek thereby to blackmail the United States into making concessions."

Nuclear Power Balance

There was scattered Far East comment on the implications of Peking's bomb for the existing U.S.-Soviet nuclear stalemate. Taipei's Central Daily News felt that Peking's latest achievement would upset the nuclear balance currently in force among the nuclear giants. The Guardian conjectured: "Chinese nuclear power could radically alter the policies of the Western nuclear nations." Yomiuri, however, did not believe China would play the nuclear deterrent game.

3

Internal Economic Pressures

Several editorials questioned whether China's current economic
level could sustain Peking's nuclear development program and, if so, at
what cost. Hong Kong's South China Morning Post advised Peking's
leaders "it would be wiser for the regime to apply such scientific and
technical resources as it possesses to the betterment of a faltering
economy." Japan's Sankei submitted that Peking's nuclear progress would
bring pressure to bear on the livelihood of the Chinese people.

Apprehension over the increasing danger to area security resulting from Communist China's "truly remarkable" speed in developing a nuclear capacity colored widespread Indian press comment on the third Chinese nuclear detonation. This was also apparent in the one available Tehran comment, which -- like most Indian dailies -- expressed fear that the test would set off a chain reaction of nuclear proliferation elsewhere and thereby play havoc with evolving plans for nuclear disarmament.

There was widespread Indian press agreement that China's increasing A-bomb capacity would increase its expansionist aims and its belligerency towards India. This has made the issue of an A-bomb for India's defense the key topic of editorials there, with opinions decidedly mixed.

Elsewhere, a Syrian editorial hailed Communist China's "huge achievement." Karachi's vernacular dailies likewise welcomed the bomb test, accepting the Chinese declaration that it would be used solely for defense. The U.S. was blamed for the test blast because of its efforts to keep Red China out of the UN. And the western nations were accused of depriving the eastern nations of nuclear secrets in order to "keep them subdued."

An Istanbul daily viewed with alarm the probability of radio-active fallout on Turkey from the Chinese bomb. Cairo papers, preoccupied with the Kosygin visit, have not yet reacted editorially to the Chinese nuclear test, but news stories about the Chinese announcement and followup stories about the nuclear fallout on Japan were played prominently on inside cable pages.

In India, need for reappraisals by Washington, Moscow and New Delhi of their nuclear policies in view of the "change in regional balance of power" received wide comment, especially in the context of India's nonnuclear bomb policy.

Indian opinion was mixed on the need for India to shift from its official position of refraining from developing its own nuclear bomb. There was an almost even division among the papers favoring an Indian A-bomb, those opposing it, and those still sitting on the fence.

A number of influential Calcutta dailies came out strongly for bomb manufacture. This also held true for New Delhi's Urdu dailies. In Madras, opinion was mixed, but <u>Andhra Prabha</u> felt that "undoubtedly,

5

nuclear weapons production by India is the only alternative" to the
present situation. The English-language press was generally more
moderate, with most favoring continuation of the "no bomb" policy.
Several, however, such as the Indian Express of New Delhi, advised
reassessments of the government's anti-bomb policy to protect India's
security interests, but cautioned against any "brash" moves.

A number of Indian dailies, in viewing the "diminishing chances"
for a test-ban treaty, spoke of the "responsibility" of the U.S. and
the USSR to provide nuclear protection for those countries not
possessing the A-bomb. This should come in a "comprehensive way"
through a "joint Soviet-American guarantee," said Dinamani of Madras
and Madurai. The Times of India expressed itself similarly, saying
that neither the U.S. nor the USSR has tried seriously to work out a
joint guarantee for India against "nuclear blackmail" by China. The
Statesman of New Delhi and Calcutta felt likewise.

The Chinese bomb test will speed nuclear proliferation and
endanger disarmament, many papers in the area said. Communist China's
A-bomb blast "will set off a chain reaction" of nuclear bomb development that may "shove all this disarmament talk down the drain," said
the Tehran Journal. Influential Hindu of Madras likewise expected
that the Chinese atomic bomb would lead other countries such as Japan
into manufacture of the bomb and pleaded for no further delay in
reaching a nonproliferation agreement.

Andhra Patrika of Madras and Vijaywada opined that China had
plans to become a world nuclear power by 1971, and that this must be
averted. Swadesamitran of Madras said that despite its claims to
the contrary, China "would be first to unleash the atom bomb," which
would probably fall on India. The Mail of Madras asserted that
Communist China was now well down the "road of nuclear blackmail"
and predicted that the U.S. "would try to play down the significance"
of the Chinese achievement. The Indian Express of Bombay said that
China was "clearly determined" to become an "operational" nuclear
power, and that the effect "psychologically and politically" of the
Chinese bomb test would be "profound" throughout the world. Statesman
of New Delhi felt similarly, but was specifically preoccupied with
China's "increased potential" for political and military "blackmail."

6

Although anticipation of Communist China's third nuclear explosion somewhat reduced its impact, it received prominent news and editorial attention in the West European press. As in the case of the two previous detonations, much of the comment focused on its political and psychological significance, particularly for China's Asian neighbors. While commentators generally sought to deflate the immediate military importance of the test, many clearly were apprehensive over the rapid strides Communist China was making in developing a nuclear weapons capability. A considerable number of papers expressed anew their oft-repeated belief that the best way to cope with the Chinese "threat" was to bring Peking into the community of nations.

Most West European papers agreed that the Chinese nuclear tests posed no immediate military threat. "There is a long and costly road from testing a weapon to having it and the means of delivering it in production," noted Copenhagen's conservative _Berlingske Tidende_. China, it continued, would probably follow a cautious foreign policy in the next several years in order not to provoke the United States into a preemptive attack upon its nuclear potential. The fact that China presently lacked a nuclear weapons delivery system, however, provided little comfort to such influential papers as _Frankfurter Allgemeine Zeitung_ which said that the time would be better used if the other atomic powers would "seriously consider how they will get the Chinese to stick to the rules of the atomic club." Britain's conservative _Birmingham Post_ similarly asserted that the important question was "what sort of neighbor will China be to the world when she does reach parity within a decade or 15 years?" For "what is immensely dangerous for world peace," it concluded, "is that China's millions are being brought up with an intense hatred of America ..."

Considerable concern was voiced that the Chinese tests would lead to an imbalance in the world's shaky nuclear equilibrium. Financial _Les Echos_ of Paris wrote that, although the latest explosion "does not yet modify the world balance of forces, the event nevertheless has a capital political significance" because it confirms China's determination "to pursue strenuously an atomic armament program which, in the long run, is bound to place People's China on an equal footing with the U.S. and Russia." West Berlin's independent _BZ_ called China a "nuclear dwarf," but added that Peking was going ahead "with great effort and cost to build weapons of terror to upset the 'equilibrium of fear' between the Soviet Union and U.S.A." Rightist _L'Aurore_ of Paris described the Chinese "bomb" as "a diplomatic weapon and an instrument of blackmail and pressure" which Peking was developing for three reasons: to attain the status of a great power, to "crack open"

7

the atomic club, and to have all colored people rally behind "the radioactive signal of the yellow bomb."

News reports that the device "contained thermonuclear material" prompted several papers to stress the apparent speed with which China was moving ahead in development of nuclear weapons. The liberal Guardian of London described the detonation as "a remarkable scientific achievement for a country still in the early stages of industrialization." Conservative Figaro, Paris, called the explosion "a nuclear leap forward" and added that China had made "fantastic progress in scarcely eighteen months." The mass circulation London Daily Mail asserted that "the estimates of how long it would take China to become fully nuclear are being hastily revised."

Observers felt that the recent Chinese test demonstrated the urgent need for an international treaty to ban the spread of nuclear weapons. Otherwise, it was argued, nations such as India and Japan would increasingly be subject to pressures to develop their own nuclear armaments. An even more prevalent theme was the feeling that the new Peking explosion underlined the importance of ending China's isolation from the world community. "The Americans will have to ask themselves," wrote pro-socialist Westfaelische Rundschau, Dortmund, "whether the policy of isolating China is still appropriate, whether China should be kept out of the UN, and whether a world power should be prevented from assuming responsibility?" This view was echoed by France's leading elite daily, Le Monde, which contended that the world must become used to reckoning with a new atomic power. "The whole effort of diplomacy, the whole pressure of public opinion," the paper said, "should tend from now on to calm down the conflicts between China and the West and to lower the walls of hatred and mutual misunderstanding." In Italy, Socialist Party organ Avanti took a similar line and declared that the Chinese experiment was "a danger signal" that tensions will increase if China continues to be ignored. The sooner the U.S. policy of isolation is abandoned, wrote independent Spandauer Volksblatt of West Berlin, "the faster China will lose its reputation of being a youngster with rude manners..." A somewhat different attitude was taken by London's conservative Daily Telegraph which argued that China's isolation was self-imposed. "Six weeks ago," the daily noted, "the U.S. declared its readiness to participate with Peking as a thermonuclear power in an effort to prevent the spread of these weapons; yesterday's big bang has been China's only answer."

8

Sensitized by the recent publicity given the forthcoming French nuclear tests, Latin American media have responded widely and adversely to the latest Communist Chinese nuclear bomb explosion. Commentaries emphasize that China is becoming a great power and a threat to humanity, and they express fear of nuclear proliferation.

In Chile, radio Emisoras Nuevo Mundo commented that "if the French experiment deserved much thought yesterday, the defense of life in Latin America is even more urgent today." Referring to the foreign policy implications, it added that "it can no longer be denied that Communist China is coming close to or may have reached the level of a great nuclear power. The fact of Communist China's development as a first-rate military power in itself weakens the power of the United States in the world."

The nuclear power theme was also stressed by Bogota's liberal El Espectador: "China continues its efforts to place itself among the so-called 'nuclear powers.' Unfortunately it is almost certain that Communist China will ignore any suggestion /to suspend tests/ which doubtless would collide with the 'nuclear eagerness' of which great powers are possessed, risking their own and the world's destruction." In a later commentary an El Espectador article noted that the West is at least partially responsible for China's present action. The article stressed that the world is "frightened" by Communist China's nuclear weapons "because it is the Communists who have them." The article recalled the plunder of China by western powers and noted with irony that a western philosophy /Marxism/ has taken root in China. "Mao is vital, fat and positive; not ascetic, thin and negative like Chiang. Along with Churchill, Mao is one of the greatest figures of modern history." The article went on to say that Mao has a "persecution complex which is understandable if China's history is reviewed. From 'a hundred flowers' an atomic rose germinates; but the seed was introduced by the West."

The Mexican press has given prominent coverage to the Chinese bomb and editorials unanimously condemned the action. The moderate Excelsior observed that "there is little value in Peking's declaration that China will not be the first to use atomic weapons, if it is taken into account that the world knows the motives that impel the atomic efforts of the Red dragon." El Heraldo (moderate), referring to the planned French tests, said, "Now Communist China boastfully announces the explosion of its first thermonuclear bomb."

9

Mexico's moderately conservative <u>Novedades</u> stressed China's "blind intransigence to the possible consequences" of its action. "There is no reason at all to justify boasting of being a nuclear power." Conservative <u>El Sol de Mexico</u> noted the "paradox" that the Chinese explosion comes at a time when the "Chinese masses are suffering extreme shortages, including food. It is surprising that western nations supply wheat to the fanatical Chinese Red regime without conditions that would impede its ominous nuclear arms race which causes anxiety to Russia, India and other Asiatic countries." The independent <u>Ovaciones</u> expressed concern over the proliferation of nuclear weapons: "As the number of atomic bomb tests increase we come closer to a nuclear war."

Lima's conservative <u>El Comercio Grafico</u> recognized that the "thermonuclear arms race is being intensified in spite of the danger to world peace and the survival of mankind. Communist China, with its defiant attitude that characterizes its policy," has exploded a third nuclear device "in less than two years." This accomplishment "indicates that in spite of the problem of underdevelopment, the Communist Chinese Government continues in its eagerness to arm itself militarily, investing funds in that program that should be used to improve the standard of living of its large population which will suffer the consequences of contamination in a large part of its territory. Consequently, radioactivity in the world has increased also and the anti-nuclear Pact of Moscow becomes inoperative. <u>With</u> <u>this</u> explosion, the one planned by France, and the underground /tests/ that are conducted by the powers that signed the Moscow Pact, recognition is given to the increased threat that Latin American people wish to see disappear for the benefit of humanity."

In Argentina, Buenos Aires' leftist tabloid <u>El Mundo</u> said that "perhaps" admission of Red China into the United Nations would be the best way of averting a major world crisis.

10

Available African media comment on the third Chinese nuclear test is limited to Tunisia and Zambia. The press coverage in Tanzania referred to it as the "first Chinese H-bomb explosion."

In Tunisia, the ruling party daily L'Action called Communist China's attempt to overtake the two nuclear superpowers a "hopeless folly" -- and one which is being pursued at the expense of the common people, "burdened with misery and backward in all domains." The editorialist also termed the big powers "irresponsible" for dissipating in an unproductive armaments race resources that could be used to solve the "real problems of our age."

"Why is the world racing toward destruction?" asked Al-Amal, L'Action's Arabic-language counterpart. The editor wondered if, after this latest nuclear explosion, the world could still delude itself with the "myth" of its search for peace.

The pro-government Times of Zambia said that the Americans and "presumably" the Russians treated the Chinese "H-bomb" with "quick contempt" because of its small size. "To ridicule Peking is short-sighted," the editorial continued, because "it is only a matter of time before they produce bigger versions ... and ... acquire the skills to deliver their bombs." The Chinese Communists' "fanatic hostility" to the rest of the world renders the appeals of Senator Robert Kennedy for some attempt at an understanding "increasingly relevant," the writer concluded.

Initial Soviet media reaction to the third Chinese nuclear test was limited, brief, and noncommittal. While Moscow promptly commented on the recent U.S. test in Nevada where radiation had escaped into the atmosphere and charged that "the tragic event has aroused a new wave of angry indignation in the world," the Chinese explosion has not yet drawn any media comment at all. Pravda, TASS, and Radio Moscow (in its domestic broadcasts) carried only brief reports summarizing the Peking announcements, including its reference to the inclusion of thermonuclear materials.

Poland, Hungary, Romania, and Bulgaria apparently followed Moscow's lead and reported the Chinese test without comment. Czechoslovak and Yugoslav media rapped the explosion, while Albania, expectedly, hailed the Chinese feat.

Prague's Rude Pravo pointed to the "negative world reaction" to the test and scored Peking for hindering Moscow's disarmament efforts. Belgrade's Borba saw a new threat to world peace in the Chinese test. "By carrying out its third nuclear experiment, China has once again ignored the interests of mankind," the daily charged. Earlier, the Yugoslav news agency TANJUG claimed that the news of the Chinese explosion "was received with indignation among the Soviet public."

Tirana also promptly commented on the Chinese test. Only three hours after the explosion, the Albanian radio informed its domestic audience of the "nuclear explosion containing thermonuclear substances in the western region of CPR." It termed the feat "a great victory for the general line of the Party in socialist construction" and "a great victory of Mao Tse-tung's ideas." Its aim "is to oppose the blackmail and nuclear threats of American imperialism and its collaborators, as well as American-Soviet cooperation to preserve the nuclear monopoly and to sabotage the revolutionary struggles of all oppressed peoples and nations."

12

On May 24, 2002, the United States and Russia signed a treaty reducing their strategic nuclear warheads to between 1,700-2,200 per nation. The treaty was the culmination of negotiations between United States President George W. Bush and Russian President Vladimar Putin (see p. 56).

"President Putin and I today ended a long chapter of confrontation, and opened up an entirely new relationship between our countries. Mr. President, I appreciate your leadership. I appreciate your vision. I appreciate the fact that we've now laid the foundation for not only our governments, but future governments to work in a spirit of cooperation and a spirit of trust. That's good. It's good for the people of Russia; it's good for the people of the United States.

"President Putin and I have signed a treaty that will substantially reduce our nuclear -- strategic nuclear warhead arsenals to the range of 1,700 to 2,200, the lowest level in decades. This treaty liquidates the Cold War legacy of nuclear hostility between our countries."

Remarks by President George W. Bush at Signing of Joint Declaration in Moscow on May 24, 2002 (released by the Office of the Press Secretary: www.whitehouse.gov)

The following is an article about the U.S-Russian nuclear arms reductions distributed by the History News Service on May 24, 2002.

U.S.-Russia Arms Reductions: History shows it is a wise act
by William Lambers

Less is more.

While this adage has not always been U.S. policy when it comes to nuclear weapons, it is the theme of the nuclear arms reductions agreement signed this week between the United States and Russia.

This new agreement will shrink the strategic nuclear arsenals of both nations to between 1,700 and 2,200 weapons apiece. According to President Bush, "The treaty will liquidate the legacy of the Cold War."

The premise of the agreement is simple: fewer armaments make more peaceful and prosperous relations. And if you flip through the pages of American history, you'll see that this approach has worked before for the United States. In fact, you'll find an interesting comparison dating back nearly 200 years.

Different times. Different weapons. But the same theme -- less is more. Naval forces on the Great Lakes played a significant role in the War of 1812. Control of the lakes was a must for any hope of victory. A massive buildup of warships on both sides played itself out in critical battles on Lake Erie and Lake Champlain. After the war had ended, naval forces from both sides still rode the waves of the Great Lakes.

After the War of 1812, John Quincy Adams was instrumental in convincing the British foreign secretary, Lord Castlereagh, that disarmament of the lakes was in the best interest of both countries. In 1817, the United States and Great Britain concluded the Rush-Bagot Agreement (named for the British minister to the

United States and acting Secretary of State Richard Rush), which demilitarized the Great Lakes and Lake Champlain by ending military shipbuilding there and calling for the disarmament of existing warships.

What better way to promote peace than to demilitarize what had been a war zone just years earlier? The agreement of 1817 was a significant step toward improved relations between the United States and Britain. Today, it is a relationship we take for granted, but in the early 1800s that relationship was one of conflict and bloodshed. Nor did the United States and Britain graduate to the friendship of today immediately following the War of 1812. The growth of their strong alliance was a gradual process of which the Rush-Bagot Agreement was a significant part.

We can see signs of a similar relationship emerging between the two great Cold War adversaries in this week's events. The legacy of the Cold War left nuclear weapons as one of its centerpieces. Both the United States and Russia accumulated stockpiles of more than 20,000 nuclear weapons during their power struggle. Fear of a nuclear holocaust hung over the world for almost 50 years.

Today, both powers hope nuclear weapons reductions will help lead to improved relations. Those relations have been strained in recent years by the U.S. withdrawal from the 1972 ABM Treaty, which prohibited missile defense, and by development of a missile defense system.

At the time of the Rush-Bagot Agreement, a statement in the Times of London read, "No wiser act was ever agreed upon than to the limitation of the naval forces on the Lakes." The same holds true for the United States and Russia today. There couldn't be a wiser act than to reduce nuclear weapons. Such an agreement establishes trust and peaceful intentions, and lays the groundwork for further nuclear arms reductions.

Just off the waters of Lake Erie, an international peace memorial stands to "inculcate the lessons of international peace by arbitration and disarmament." The waters of Lake Erie are calm now, far removed from the fierce naval battles of the War of 1812. We know that the Rush-Bagot Agreement was one with long-lasting and positive implications. Only time will tell what the impact of the U.S. and Russian agreements on nuclear arms will be. We can only hope that another peace memorial will somewhere stand one day in honor of these Russian-American efforts.

William Lambers is a writer for the History News Service and the author of Nuclear Weapons (2002)

Glossary

Atomic Bomb -- nuclear weapon first developed by the United States and used on the Japanese cities of Hiroshima and Nagasaki to end World War II.

Comprehensive Test Ban Treaty (CTBT) -- treaty banning all nuclear test explosions or any other nuclear explosion. Treaty has not taken effect as of 2001.

Hydrogen bomb -- nuclear weapon developed in the 1950's, far more powerful than the atomic bomb.

ICBM -- Intercontinental Ballistic Missile

INF Treaty -- Intermediate Range Nuclear Forces Treaty signed in 1987 eliminating intermediate and shorter range missiles for both the Soviet Union and the United States.

International Atomic Energy Agency (IAEA) -- organization dedicated to the peaceful uses of nuclear energy.

IRBM -- Intermediate Range Ballistic Missile

Limited Test Ban Treaty -- 1963 treaty that banned nuclear test explosions or any other nuclear explosion in the atmosphere, underwater and in outer space.

MRBM -- Medium Range Ballistic Missile

Nuclear Non-Proliferation Treaty (NPT) -- treaty establishing five nuclear weapons nations, China, Great Britain, France, Russia and the United States. All other nations signing the treaty are prohibited from developing nuclear weapons. The five nuclear powers cannot assist any nation in producing nuclear weapons and are committed to ultimately eliminating their own nuclear stockpiles.

Nuclear warheads -- nuclear bomb deliverable via missile or other delivery method.

Nuclear weapons – weapons of mass destruction such as the atomic bomb and the hydrogen bomb.

INDEX